DORSET
FOOD

Tess ready to milk with her stool and bucket. Wood engraving by Vivien Gribble for the 1926 edition of Thomas Hardy's Tess of the D'Urbervilles.

DORSET
FOOD

JO DRAPER

SUTTON PUBLISHING

First published in 1988 by
The Dovecote Press Ltd

This new edition published in 2007 by
Sutton Publishing Limited · Phoenix Mill · Thrupp
Stroud · Gloucestershire · GL5 2BU

British Library Cataloguing in Publication Data
A catalogue record for this book is available from the British Library.

ISBN 978-0-7509-4458-8

To Rebecca,
with love and gratitude

A fair at Dorchester, c. 1800. (Author's collection)

Contents

Introduction

[In Dorset] there is no want of any Thing, that is necessary for the Maintenance and Support of Man; since both Sea and Land seem to vie with each other, and strive which shall indulge his Appetite most, and yield the greatest Abundance. To All this we must add, that its fine Beer and Ale are universally admired, and by some preferred before the Wines of France.

And as it abounds thus with Provisions of all sorts, which are to be procured likewise at very reasonable Rates, it is no great Wonder, that such a Number of Families, even of high Distinction, make it their favourite Place of Abode.

('The Natural History of Dorsetshire', *Universal Magazine*, 1757)

Eighteenth-century writers all remark on the fecundity of the county, its mutton, shellfish, cheese, butter, fish, and so on. The cooks in the county had an abundance to work with, some of it sadly now gone, like the oysters of Poole and Purbeck or the gigantic catches of mackerel formerly caught between Weymouth and Lyme Regis.

This abundance of foodstuffs was not shared by all the inhabitants of the county. The upper classes, the gentry and most of the farmers ate well, but sadly the bulk of the population, the farm labourers, ate little of the produce of their labour.

THE LABOURER'S FOOD

Few of the recipes here come from cottages: in the eighteenth and nineteenth centuries labourers' wages were too small to allow for any elaboration in cooking. However, they were the largest section of the population.

Even in the middle of the nineteenth century, when some mechanisation had taken place, nearly a third of all males over ten in the county were agricultural labourers. The analysis of the 1851 census also shows a tenth of rural men as farmers, graziers or their relatives, and probably many of these were little better off than the labourers. In contrast to the 22,864 male agricultural labourers, there were only 180 male landed proprietors and 83 independent gentlemen. Four thousand women were described as agricultural labourers or indoor farm servants, dividing nearly equally between the two categories. These are probably only the full-time female agricultural workers, with many more working part-time. Dorset labourers' wages were notoriously low, partly because there was so little industry in the county to compete for their labour.

The bare and poor interior of a Dorset labourer's cottage in 1846, as seen in the Illustrated London News.

One of the earliest detailed accounts of a labourer's diet is from Durweston near Blandford in 1795, part of Sir F.M. Eden's investigation into the state of the poor. A 52 year old labourer and his four children had an income of about 7s a week, with the house rent paid by the parish. 'The usual breakfast of the family is tea, or bread and cheese, their dinner and supper, bread and cheese, or potatoes sometimes mashed with fat taken from broth, and sometimes salt alone. Bullock's cheek is generally bought every week to make broth. Treacle is used to sweeten tea instead of sugar. Very little milk or beer is used.'

Subsequent reports are as bleak: Stevenson in his *General View of the Agriculture of the County of Dorset* (1815) discusses the labourer under the general heading of the Poor, using the terms as interchangeable. Labourers were being paid 6s or 7s a week, when corn cost that amount a bushel. 'About a bushel of wheat is consumed in a week by a man and his wife and three children . . . the poor are sometimes accused of unnecessary wastefulness, in making cakes without yeast, and broiling or baking them on a gridiron, by which means it is said the quantity is lessened.' This seems pig-headedly unrealistic and cruel today. The farmers were making huge profits because of high prices, and paying the labourers barely enough to keep them from starvation. The same sort of attitude continues through the nineteenth century. Dr Aldridge, for example, said in 1869:

a great deal might be done to improve the diet of the labouring man by the ladies of the district teaching the labourer's wife how to make the best use of the food which a kind providence has bestowed upon them, as well as pointing out to them that which is most nutritious and within their limited means. A clergyman (eight miles off) assured me that he had seen a piece of uncooked mutton, supplied to a labourer's wife, thrown under the table for the cat to eat. She did not know how to cook it.

Stevenson thought the labourers' lot had been much improved by the introduction of potatoes, 'scarcely known thirty years since'. At that time 'the labourers had very little beside bread and cheese and water, but at present they have the important additions of potatoes, pork and bacon'. However 'on parts of the Vale of Blackmoor, the peasantry eat very little besides bread and skim-milk cheese'. Elsewhere 'many of the poor keep two or three fowls; and they generally have ovens and plenty of fuel, to enable them to make use of the economical method of baking their own bread'.

The reformer John Bright recorded the wages and expenditure of labourers around Sherborne in 1844, finding wages varying from 6s to 9s a week. Even with additional earnings at harvest or children at work many families had to manage on less than 10s a week. Bright recorded details of eighty-two labourers' budgets in north and east Dorset, and most spent half or more of the total family earnings on bread. This was supplemented by potatoes, grown by the labourer, and Bright noted that 'about 25 years ago, Barley was a common article of diet in times of scarcity . . . A Barley Cake made of barley meal, with an apple or onion and lard, might often be seen, but is scarcely ever eaten now.'

In 'A Lay to Dorset' published in 1831 the Revd W.M. Smith Marriott displays a contemporary Arcadian view of the poor's food:

> Look at the Shepherd-boy who tends
> Upon the downs his fleecy friends,
> He never sees a costly meal,
> No fancied wants 'tis his to feel;
> A crust is all he has to eat,
> With hunger's sauce to make it sweet.
> Ah! when the rich who daily see
> Their table spread so sumptuously,
> And e'en midst plenty's self, regret
> That something more is wanted yet,
> When they his healthy features trace
> Oft envy him his rosy face.
> No downy pillow rests his head,
> But on an humble pallet bed
> 'Tis his no watchful hours to keep
> For scarce laid down he's fast asleep.

The shepherd boy was unlikely to get the chance to eat 'his fleecy friends'. Bright met a butcher in 1844 who said he 'scarcely ever sold any meat to labourers, except perhaps 3 or 4 pounds, two or three times a year in the whole village. Or where a sheep happened to be killed, which was giddy [ie. ill], when the meat tho' it was quite wholesome, was sold cheaper than common. Bacon was he said the only meat they consumed, and of this 1lb a week was quite as much as they could afford.' Bread, potatoes and cheese were the staples all through the nineteenth century for the labourers. Rachel Hayward of Stourpaine, giving evidence to the 1843 inquiry into the employment of women and children in agriculture is typical: she had a bushel of wheat a week, potatoes and a few vegetables, buying each week '¾lb of soap, 1oz of tea, ½lb of bacon. I reckon we eat a pound of bread each day; that, with potatoes, gives us enough'.

In 1867 a Dorset farmer reported his labourers' diet to the local paper: 'bread and cheese, much of the former, a little of the latter; at night for supper some hot potatoes and a slice of fried fat pork, also some very small beer provided by the farmer' (small beer means weak beer). One of his labourers said, 'There are eleven of us (baby included) and we consume in bread and puddings 5 pecks [about 14lb to a peck] of flour weekly, equal of 20 4lb loaves, and we could eat more.' A peck of flour then cost 3s, so he was spending 15s a week on flour alone out of a wage of 14s 6d (the earnings of his three eldest children helped here). (*Bridport News*, 14 September 1867)

In 1868 when a second inquiry was held there was no improvement in the labourer's food. On average, the commission suggested the labourer 'has for his breakfast bread and Dorset cheese, called by him "choke-dog", and a cup of coffee; for dinner a rasher of bacon and vegetables, and coffee again; and for supper probably a rasher of bacon and fried potatoes'. Compared to the evidence given them by labourers' wives, this seems rather hopeful. A shepherd's wife from near Blandford is typical: 'Last winter we got but a very little after we'd had our bread.'

Villagers by the sea were always better off, as fish was freely available. *The Penny Magazine for the Society for the Diffusion of Useful Knowledge* found, when their correspondent visited Portland in 1837, that despite the small earnings of the quarrymen (7s–9s a week) and the large families 'they are both well fed and well clothed'. Vegetable plots of an acre each were common, producing corn, potatoes and vegetables. 'In this way flour for the puddings, potatoes for the winter store . . . and a good supply of small fruits and esculent vegetables' was supplied. A cow was often kept on the common land: 'Milk is consequently cheap and abundant, and home-made cheeses are found on most tables.' There were many chicken, and therefore eggs, and mushrooms in great abundance. 'Fish of every sort abounds, and is sold at low prices fresh from the sea.'

WORKHOUSE FOOD

Food in the workhouse is often seen as the worst possible, mean in quality and quantity. In fact no one starved there, and people did starve outside. The published diet sheets seem short on fruit and vegetables, otherwise providing an adequate but very plain diet. Cerne Abbas Union in 1838 is typical. An able-bodied man had 6oz of bread (about 6 slices) and 1½ pints of gruel for breakfast; 4oz cooked meat and 1½ pints of soup and 6oz potatoes for dinner; and 6oz of bread with 1½ pints of broth for supper. Four nights a week there was 2oz of cheese for supper, and only on Fridays a pudding with dinner, either rice or suet. Anyone under 60, female, or a child had a smaller allowance, but those over 60 had extra each week 1oz of tea, 4oz of butter and 5oz of sugar.

In a letter addressed to the Guardian of the Dorchester Union in 1844 a complainant stated, 'I imagine the diet of our Union at the present time, to be somewhat superior to that obtainable by many Independant Labourers.' This was probably true although the Poor Law Commissioner's instructions were 'on no account must the dietary of the workhouse be superior or equal to the ordinary mode of subsistence of the labouring classes of the neighbourhood'.

The state of the labouring classes in Dorset in 1844 was bleakly summarised by E.C. Tufnell in a report preserved in the Peel papers. 'In a great part of this district wages are so low, that they cannot fall, and the distress of the country does not affect the labouring classes. Their *normal* state is one of the deepest privation, to lower which should be to depopulate the land.'

The earlier parish poorhouses and workhouses were less regimented and James Frampton's recommendations for Wool workhouse in 1797 were economical enough, but show rather more feeling. 'The poor to have meat one day in the week, on Sundays . . . the other days Potatoes and other garden stuff, Bread, gruel with flour and salt and treacle, Milk, Porridge, Rice, and sometimes a Red Herring with the Potatoes, which is very savoury and cheap, as a little goes a long way, and no salt required. If bread fried hard in lard is put in their gruel, it has the same effect, though may require salt. No butter or cheese allowed with the Bread. No small Beer. . . . Milk if it can be got reasonable, is a great advantage to the Poor. Ginger is very cheap and wholesome for old people, as it very warm and to the taste pleasant.' He thought the inmates should have good fires and good blankets.

Red herrings were simply smoked herrings, but the direction to fry bread and put it in the gruel (porridge) sounds very odd.

FARMHOUSE FOOD

Rural cooking immediately suggests farmhouse food: lavish plain dishes, made from fresh ingredients. The London playwright John O'Keefe spent six weeks of the summer in 1791 in West Lulworth, staying at the Red Lion, which had its own farm.

A Dorset farmyard in the 1890s, with chicken, cattle, a wagon and half barrels for water and food.

For lunch he had 'roast loin of lamb, delicate boiled chickens, green-peas, young potatoes, a gooseberry pie, thick cream, good strong home-brewed ale, and a glass of tolerable port-wine'. For supper 'the Lulworth-staple, lobster and crabs, to which was added, cold lamb and cucumbers, gooseberry pie, butter, milk, and bread'. For breakfast 'Suchong tea, sugar, honey, cream, milk, home-made bread, and rolls, butter and eggs'.

In the late nineteenth century the farmhouse was seen as the home of traditional cooking. Jane Panton recalled the kitchen of North Farm near Wareham in the 1870s:

Three Dorset milkers in 1911, with artistically arranged aprons.

There were always great hams and flitches of bacon suspended from the kitchen ceiling from enormous hooks; mutton and beef, chickens and ducks were grown on the place; great bowls of cream and baskets of eggs and pounds of butter filled the shelves in the delightful inner dairy, and the bread was made from wheat threshed out on the barn-floor by hand, with the good old flails. The bread was made and baked at home in a brick oven, and I recollect it being put to rise in front of the fire overnight in a vast earthenware crock, covered by a linen cloth. . . . Very early in the morning it was put in square tins in the oven, which had been heated with enormous bundles of furze cut from the uplands . . . it required vast stores [of furze] to heat the yawning brick oven, in which not only was the bread baked, but a good deal of other cooking done at the same time. London housekeepers smile at the old-fashioned receipts which begin 'Take a dozen eggs and a quart of cream', but at the North Farm these directions were carried out without a qualm.

Specifying that the wheat had been threshed with a flail rather than by a machine suggests she could taste the difference.

Llewelyn Powys celebrated Dorset farmhouse cooking in the 1930s:

One week it is the time for duck and green peas, the next week it is Whit Sunday and the little rosy-checked maid has supplied the cool larder with a large cooking basin of green fruit as hard as bullets, all ready, headed and tailed, for the first gooseberry tart. Now the weeks have come when the willow pattern plates, grown dim with age and use, are piled high with broad beans in their grey coats! Then again it is the blackberry season and there stands on the sideboard a huge jug of fresh autumn cream to mix with the delicious juices of these 'wild grapes' that were gathered after school by the children of the village from the long green hazel nut hedges.

(*Wessex Memories*, 2003)

PICNICS

Seldom recorded, but fashionable from the late eighteenth century, picnics in Dorset's varied countryside have been a pleasure for 200 years. The *Dorset County Chronicle* (29 July 1843) record 'Pic Nics – These delightful summer recreations are now becoming quite fashionable. . . . Few places can boast of more suitable and retired spots' or such delightful cruises. Osmington, Lulworth and Portland are 'well known to the consumers of prawns, lobsters or crabs', those places 'being famous for these luxuries'. The word picnic seems to be used to mean going to eat at Lulworth etc., rather than taking one's own food.

That was for upper-class Weymouth visitors: a more democratic 1862 picnic was described by the *Dorset County Chronicle* (14 August 1842) when thousands of local people visited a rural fete at Hambledon Hill: in one place 'a gigantic plum cake, there a basket of slice bread and butter, kept in countenance with a basin of boiled eggs and a few shellfish, then a pigeon pie, a few little tarts, then sandwiches and sausages, besides, perhaps, a cold ham or a little truckle cheese of their own making'. Picnics don't change much, although pigeon pie or cheese of one's own making are less common today.

ROYAL FOOD

The peak of aristocratic cooking in Dorset might be expected to have been when George III stayed at Weymouth. He came for summer holidays most years between 1789 and 1805, transforming Weymouth from a small bathing resort to one of the most fashionable. However, he was a plain-living king, known as Farmer George, and his appetite was not costly. By the time he had started coming to Weymouth his illness had started and he lived simply. In 1801, at Kew just before he came on to Weymouth, his regime was recorded: 'Plain dishes, as roast mutton, lamb, veal, beef, and fowls, generally cold, with salads, is the diet of the royal family: made dishes are never touched. The King's beverage is wine considerably diluted with water.'

Details of one meal King George ate in 1799 were recorded by his anxious hostess. The whole party, five royals and their entourage, turned up unexpectedly at Wollaston House, Dorchester. They walked round the town, then the lady of the house, Mrs Mary Frampton, recollected: 'I conducted them into my eating-room, trembling lest the Collation should not be as it ought, but really it was as well prepared as could be

Satirical drawing of George III, 1791. He is toasting muffins on an open fire, a common cooking method but not one expected from a king.

expected on so short a notice – cold partridges, cold meat of different sorts, and removes of mutton-chops and fruit – tea at the side table. Mary made tea, Mr Damer carried it to them and I waited on the Majesties as they ate, and Mary on the princesses.' Besides the king, queen and three princesses, five other ladies partook of the meal.

A long poem, 'The Royal Tour and Weymouth Amusements' (1795) published as by Peter Pindar, but actually by John Wolcot, the most prolific of four or five contemporary satirical writers using that name, makes fun of the royal family's economical habits:

> The Mail arrives! Hard! Hard! The cheerful horn,
> To MAJESTY announcing oil and corn;
> Turnips and cabbages, and soup and candles;
> And lo, each article GREAT CAESAR handles!
> Bread, cheese, salt, catchup, vinegar and mustard,
> Small beer and bacon, apple-pie and custard;
> All, all from WINDSOR greets his frugal GRACE,
> For WEYMOUTH is a d–mn'd expensive place.

We know that while he was in Weymouth King George enjoyed Radipole biscuits at The Honest Man Inn, Radipole, and a good pudding at the Portland Arms,

THE ROYAL
PORTLAND ARMS HOTEL,
IN THE ISLAND OF PORTLAND

A. HINDMARSH,
GRANDSON OF THE LATE MRS. GIBBS,
Proprietor.

His late Majesty George III. once during every season of his Royal Visits to Weymouth, honored the "Portland Arms," and on these occasions Mrs. Gibbs had the honor of serving up the King's dinners, and of which His Majesty condescended to express his approbation, more particularly of the **ROYAL PUDDING** she then introduced, and which he caused to be advertized.

When His late Royal Highness Prince Albert laid the foundation stone of the Portland Breakwater, a splendid luncheon was prepared for His Royal Highness and Suite, at which the **ROYAL PUDDING**, (made from the same recipe) occupied a prominent position, and with which His Royal Highness was pleased to express his great gratification.

AT THE HOTEL MAY BE SEEN

THE REIVE POLE,
Which exhibits the ancient Saxon method of keeping Accounts.

THE REIVE COURT IS HELD AT THIS HOUSE.

Queen Charlotte grilling sprats on an open fire. The drawing is intended to show how mean the king and queen were, but illustrates the way many people cooked.

King George's Pudding still being advertised in the early nineteenth century.

Fortuneswell, which was afterwards, by permission, named Royal Pudding and much demanded by other visitors, but maddeningly there is not even a hint in the contemporary documents as to the recipe for either.

A Weymouth visitor who ate at the Portland Arms in 1866 recorded the event, and the pudding, in verse:

At Portland Arms we did alight, told Mrs. H. our fun,
When she chimed in 'I'm glad you're back, for dinner is just done.'
The dinner it was quickly served, a leg of Portland mutton
And fowl (which was by no means foul) enough to please a glutton.
And reader do forgive me for making this bad pun,
Which truly is excusable, for the mutton was not done!
So then we eat some bacon, served up with nice French beans,
And finished off with pudding, called here the 'King's and Queen's;' *
Now having dined thus sumptuously, and washed it down with sherry,
We ordered round the carriage, and for starting did get ready.

The twinkle refers the reader to the card of the hotel (opposite). Bacon and 'nice French beans' sounds very modern, somehow, as does the 'ale and bread and cheese' they had earlier eaten at the same inn for lunch. (*Our Trip to Weymouth in the Summer of '66*) (DCL)

WILD HARVEST

In the past almost every wild plant that is not poisonous has been gathered and eaten, particularly in times of famine, when even couch grass roots were ground and cooked. Medieval pottages or soups contained herbs as well as vegetables, and young leaves of many plants were used for salads. A few plants were particularly associated with the county.

Sea Kale 'Sea Kail, or Beach-kail, which is a rough hard plant, as it grows wild on the cliffs near Burton and elsewhere, has been introduced into garden culture in this county, and is now become very common in the gardens of the principal farmers, and is much esteemed, it being a winter vegetable, sometimes in use as early as Christmas.' (Stevenson, 1815) Mrs Machin's recipe is earlier, and must be for the tough wild stuff: 'To Dress Sea Keale: Wash very clean in Six Pails of water then put it into a large pot of water let ye Boyl with a good handful of salt before you put the Keale in then boyle ye Keale half an hour.' Presumably it was the spring shoots of the sea kale which were eaten like sprouting broccoli.

Sea Holly These prickly plants seem unlikely to be edible, but from at least the seventeenth century the root was candied to make an expensive sweet-meat called eringoe, and considered aphrodisiac. Mrs Machin's recipe book of 1709 has a recipe to candy it, but by the later eighteenth century it was less popular, and at Tyneham it is only included in one medicinal recipe.

Wild Arum 'A woman of this isle [Portland] obtained a reward from the Society of Arts, for the discovery that starch may be profitably extracted from the common herb *arum* or cuckow pint . . . the starch obtained from the *arum* looks very white, and may be afforded at 10*d* a pound.' Stevenson recorded this small but profitable crop in 1815, and perhaps the discovery was made during the wars with France in the late eighteenth and early nineteenth centuries, when imported arrowroot would have been difficult to obtain. Some herbals call it Portland sago, and it was still being gathered from the fallow fields on Portland in 1837 'in unparalleled abundance . . . the roots are gathered by the women, the farinaceous matter is extracted, and a fine supply of British arrowroot is secured' (*Penny Magazine*). Like true arrowroot it was used to make blancmange.

Cabbage Dorset is supposed to have a particular association with cabbage, since, according to some authorities, Sir Anthony Ashley of Wimborne St Giles introduced

Bunching watercress at Doddings, 1961.
(Jesty collection)

cabbages to Britain from Holland. He died in 1628, and his effigy in Wimborne St Giles church has a facetted globular object at his feet, which has been taken to be a cabbage. Sir Anthony may have introduced one particular type of cabbage, but not the whole race. They are commonplace in recipes from the medieval period, and were cultivated in this country from the time of the Romans.

Rock Samphire Rock Samphire was found 'in the crevices of the cliffs in Portland, and on the Purbeck coast, especially about Tineham; from whence great quantities are collected for pickling', according to Richard Pultney in about 1800. The Tyneham cookery book has a recipe for it:

TO PICKLE SAMPHIRE
Green it over a gentel fire close cover'd with good Vinegar and a bit of Alum and a little salt, so let it stand to be cold then take the Liquor from it and boyl it up quick put it on it scald hot cover it so let it stand till fit for use, do it in a bell mettle pot or skillet.

Mrs L.M.G. Bond recollected that at Tyneham before the Second World War 'Samphire appeared on the table on one or two occasions for the benefit of an enquiring guest but met with scant appreciation. One such who had spent long periods in Morocco remarked that the pickle tasted like the smell of camels.'

Watercress The wild watercress must always have been gathered from the chalk streams of Dorset: it grows wherever the river water has a high calcium content. The best and earliest was found around springs because the water temperature was warmer there and the mineral level higher. The wild plant would have been harvested in spring and autumn, and must have been particularly welcomed in early spring, when other greenstuffs were in short supply.

Watercress occurs only rarely in Dorset recipe books, but there is a medicinal recipe in the Tyneham one:

SPRING JUICES
Juice of brook Lime Water Cresses Scurvy Grass Each 1 pint Juices of Sevel Oranges sp: mix these together then bottle it and Take ½ a pint every morning this is to be made the latter end of February.

Scurvy grass is coastal; brooklime and watercress would have been found in streams. All three would have been gathered around Tyneham. This is an eighteenth-century attempt at vitamin pills.

Commercial watercress growing started only in the early nineteenth century in Kent and spread to Hertfordshire later that century. This is the furthest north watercress will grow. The Dorset industry started in 1890 and used the railway network to supply the Midlands and north. Prepared beds, floored with gravel, were constructed where there were springs, and were carefully protected from ordinary river water. Originally there were the two peaks of spring and autumn production, as with the wild growth, but greater understanding of the requirements of the plants (e.g. the adjusting of the levels of zinc and phosphate in the water with natural additives) combined with growing the plants successively from seed and protecting them when necessary with plastic covers means that watercress is now cut all year round. Dorset produces one-third of British watercress, from 24 acres of beds. Approximately 45,000lb (20,000 kilos) are harvested each year in the county, being sent to market daily.

The plant anchors itself in the gravel of the beds, but feeds entirely from the spring water. The flavour varies: it is 'hotter' in the winter, giving a fine flavour for soups. Watercress makes a good addition to any salad, and is tasty with bread and cheese.

SHOPPING AND HOUSEKEEPING
The difference between eighteenth-century (and earlier) housekeeping and shopping and today's is summarised in respective bacon recipes: earlier ones start 'take one fine hog' and proceed to kill, joint and preserve it, whereas our recipe would merely ask for half a pound of back rashers, or a neat joint.

Delivery at Rendall's grocery, Lyme Regis, c. 1900. On the left is a formal photograph from an advertisement; the other is taken by Rendall himself, looking along the passage behind the shop and giving a more informal image. (Lyme Regis Museum)

In the past food had less to do with shopping. In the eighteenth and nineteenth centuries the farmers or owners of large estates obtained most of their food from the estate or farm, and the labourers had too little money to shop much. Only the middle classes, particularly those who lived in towns, shopped for the bulk of their food.

The household book belonging to Edward Weld of Lulworth Castle for 1743 survives, and shows purchases of exotics like coffee, tea, chocolate, pepper, sugar and wine, alongside herrings and saltfish, wheat, pease and sage, but clearly all the flour, meat, vegetables, milk, cheese and butter, and much of the fish was coming from the estate.

The household account book which survives from Loders is valuable because a very large proportion of the food was purchased and so recorded. Vegetables only seem to occur when large quantities, such as a hundredweight of French beans, were acquired to preserve them for the winter. Rabbit, pheasant and other game are virtually absent (two wood pigeons and a woodcock for 6*d* is one exception), and eggs are never bought. Everything else is there, if seasonally. Milk is particularly regular: purchases of milk, cheese and butter start in late April, peak in September and then fall off. A sample summer week, starting 7 July 1761:

For 2 Bushs of Wheat	8	8
For 6lbs of Butter	2	9
For milk		1½
A Qr and Breast of Veal	2	1
For 2 Pieces of Beef of Br. Travers	4	0
A Leg of Mutton	1	3
For 2 Dozn of Mackral	0	8
A Peck of Salt	1	3
For Salt Peter	0	6
Half an oz of Nutmegs	0	4
For 4lb and ½ of Turkey Currants	1	0
A Bundle of Carrots	0	1½

The total for the week is £1 2s 9d, part of a year which cost £56 7s 1¾d, not including the 'cyder' or beer. Sometimes the price per pound for meat is given, so that one can estimate that during the week 10lb of veal, 32lb of beef and 6lb of mutton was purchased. The salt and saltpetre indicates that bacon is about to be made, and the next week there it is: 'half a Pig 94lbs at 2½lb'. 2 bushels of wheat were bought most weeks of the year, enough to make twelve 9lb loaves after it was ground into flour.

A page from the Loders accounts book for November 1761: sugar at 6d a pound, mutton 2d a pound.

The market at Weymouth in 1790, with butchers' small stalls in the background.

The accounts cover eleven years from 1751, the careful handwriting steadily listing thousands of items, and they only cease because the book was full. Many of the ingredients needed for the recipes in the eighteenth-century cookery books occur, such as breast of mutton perhaps cooked in similar style to the recipe from Tyneham.

Even early in the twentieth century at Tyneham the farm (and sea) supplied the meat, fish and all the other perishable foods needed. L.M.G. Bond recalled the food shopping in her book *Tyneham*:

The store-room proffered a delicious blend of appetising smells, for here my Mother kept her housekeeping supplies. Once in each quarter one of the farm waggons, the team decked out with all their ribbons and brasses and with the 'rumblers' gaily chiming in their frame above the shaft mare's collar, would journey over the hill to Wareham station and bring back a full load of cases from the Army and Navy Stores. We – not unwillingly – were pressed into the important business of unpacking the cases, checking their contents by the invoices and stowing the goods away in their appointed places. Huge packages of candied peel, sultanas, raisins, currants, almonds, sugarloaf, candied, demerara, crystallised, moist, caster, granulated, icing – of coffee, tea and cereals were opened and decanted into earthenware or tin containers. The 7-lb tins of biscuits filled the space behind the door from floor to ceiling and regiments of jam-pots, bottles and jars were ranged in order on the shelves. All kinds of sauces, pickles and condiments, crystallised fruits and skins of glazing, pastes, potted meats and spices, nutmegs, chillis, isinglass, sardines and anchovies took their accustomed places. Chests on the floor accommodated soap and candles, brushes, dusters, swabs and floor cloths, blacking, polishes and knife powder, with leathers, saddle soap and sponges for the stable. I took some time, when I was married, to get accustomed to the hand-to-mouth idea of housekeeping in town, which still appears to me improvident and wasteful. The full shelves of the Tyneham storeroom gave a sense of orderly preparedness and, save for stock-taking and ordering once a quarter, there was no need to worry about shopping, the constantly recurring burden of today.

Mary Horsfall wrote recollections of holidaying in Bridport from 1898 to 1918, and recorded that 'visitors from London who wanted the choice and quality meats they were used to at home, did not appreciate the tough Dorset mutton, and it was a welcome and enterprising stroke when Mrs Draper at a small grocery shop in East Street introduced New Zealand lamb'. This is not how we see shopping in 1900 – frozen lamb better than Dorset lamb?

FARMERS' ORDINARIES
Ordinaries were fixed-price (and usually fixed-menu) meals provided by inns or taverns, and farmers' ordinaries were the lunches provided by those places on market days for farmers who virtually only came to town that day.

Many of the inns were simple, like that described in Hardy's *Woodlanders*: 'a long, low apartment, with a sanded floor herring-boned with a broom, a wide red-curtained window to the street . . . the front part full of a mixed company of dairymen and butchers'. The hero had eaten his lunch there on market days for twenty years, but the mincing heroine, educated above her station, is shocked by its being simple and humble with a 'well scrubbed settle . . . narrow table with its knives and steel forks, tin pepper boxes, salt-cellars, and posters advertising the sale of bullocks'.

Annual Christmas dinners were also held, and enthusiastically reported by the local paper. The 1905 Christmas Market Dinner at The Junction, Dorchester, organised by the chairman of the ordinary, had so many customers that there were two sittings. The menu concentrated on meat: 'Soup: Oxtail. Fish: Turbot and lobster, fillet of sole and anchovy sauce. Joints: Sirloin of Beef, roast and boiled beef, and boiled mutton. Poultry: Roast turkey and goose. Game: roast pheasant. Sweets: Plum pudding, mince pies, apple tart and custard and wine jellies. Cheese and celery.' All, according to the paper, 'of the choicest quality, cooked to a turn, and served properly

A west Dorset 'refreshment room' or café, 1890s. The original caption is 'Cottage at Eype'. (Bridport Museum)

and piping hot'. 'Sherry and champagne, claret and port were supplied liberally.' One hopes that all market business had been concluded before that lot.

These dinners seem to have followed a distinct pattern: the Milborne St Andrew Farmers' club met at the King's Arms at Christmas 1906 and ate 'Thick oxtail, consommé Julienne, Boiled cod sauce Cardinal, fried fillet of sole, roast haunch of mutton red currant jelly, boiled legs of mutton caper sauce, roast sirloins of beef, horseradish, roast turkey and ham. Roast pheasants and chip potatoes, roast haunch of venison. Apple tarts and custard, wine jellies, blancmanges. Cheese, celery, dessert.'

Apart from a trifle more French in the menu, it was a very similar meal to that offered by the Junction.

A few other meals at Dorset inns or hotels were recorded, not always with pleasure. F.J.H. Darton reviled the changes in Dorset inns over twenty-five years. In the 1890s he and some friends ate at the Red Lion, Lyme Regis: 'for 2s 6d each we ate (i) dressed crab, lots and lots of it; (ii) Easter lamb, the real Dorset lamb; (iii) a fruit tart of surpassing excellence; (iv) Blue Vinney in good condition and in its proper state – a whole cheese'. Twenty-five years later the bar-parlour had been converted to a lounge and 'it appeared that only cold beef could be obtained. But the pickles therewith were of an abhorrent type, and the only salad was a cucumber.' The sweets were prunes and rice or stewed plums, and the only cheese was Cheddar from Harrod's *(The Marches of Wessex)*.

Sometimes customers complained because they were getting older, and could not cope with the meals they had eaten in the past. William Macready, the great actor, recorded in his diary that he dined at Weymouth in 1850, and it only cost 5s, whereas in 1815 with a friend they had eaten 'small haddock, leg of Portland mutton, small apple tart, almonds and raisins, bottle of port, bottle of madeira', and the bill was nearly £3. Young appetites. Weymouth hotels were not always good: Joseph Faringdon, the artist, kept a diary of his tour in 1809, and complained that at Stacey's Hotel, Weymouth, 'Extortion seems to be carried as far as it can go.' He and his companion had for supper 'Bread 1d, Pint of very bad port 3d, Roast chicken 3d, Mutton chops 3d, French beans Potatoes and butter 2d, Sallad, 1d and tart 3d': 1s 4d for a supper for two does not seem expensive but 'the character of the House was expressed in dishes put upon the table. The Fowl had been stripped of such parts as could be taken away, and the wine we could not drink.' Certainly they fared better elsewhere.

FEASTS AND FESTIVALS

Festive food tended to be seasonal or expensive, sometimes both. Ralph Wightman remembered the harvest suppers of about 1900.

> In those bad old days of the early part of the century the farm workers' wages were very low. He could afford very little meat, but what he did buy was English; and when he went out to supper he expected not only the best, but plenty of it. The food, then, at the Harvest Home supper consisted of vast joints of cold meat. There was always a home cured ham with the fat three inches thick, there was a huge joint of boiled salt beef, and a lordly roast sirloin. For some reason or other mutton and lamb were not popular, and I suppose poultry were too expensive for the farmer to provide. The only mention I remember of poultry was of 'poor men's goose', which was a fresh leg of pork, stuffed with sage and onions and roasted.
>
> The main eating at the harvest supper was slabs from these noble joints, followed by a second and third helping. There were piles of hot floury steaming potatoes to go with the meat, and each dish of potatoes was crowned with a fast vanishing chunk of butter. To top up everything and clean the palate there was locally made cheese.

As meat was too expensive for the labourers, liberal quantities of it, plainly cooked, made for a feast. In the middle of the agricultural riots of the 1830s the

Journal of Mary Frampton records the Christmas feast in the big house at Moreton. 'The peacock in full plumage with its fiery mouth was placed on the dinner table, with of course the boar's head . . . the hare appeared with the red herrings astride its back, and the wassail bowl and lamb's wool were not inferior to former years.' Here more exotic foods were needed to make a feast, as meat was everyday food.

Lyme Corporation dinners in the early eighteenth century also star different sorts of meat – in October 1727 they ate 'A ham 6 large foules 8*s*; a pees of Rost Beef 5*s*: a Large moton pie 5*s*; bread and pickells 2*s*'; total for food £1, washed down with 31 'Botells of wine' costing £3 2*s*.

The first annual feast of the reconstituted Society of Dorset Men in London is particularly interesting as 'various items of the *menu* were reminiscent of the home county'. Two hundred and thirty-six members and guests ate on 27 February 1905 'Portland mutton, the excellent Dorset pudding – a delicate confection of apples, prepared from a *recipe* obtained form Dorset especially for the occasion . . . the watercress, such as grows in profusion in the freshest streams of Dorset, the cider, and, not least though last, the "blue vinney" cheese, which piquant delicacy, when brought in, was greeted with a great and sustained cheer.' The food perceived as Dorset fare in 1905 is similar to that of today, except the Portland mutton, now unobtainable. I think the apple pudding was an apple cake.

In the 1930s Llewelyn Powys considered Dorset food:

If I were to be asked what particular food was characteristic of Dorset I should suggest mutton, though the celebrated Portland breed (albeit Portland lamb is still sold in the London markets) has for a long time become extinct. Next to Dorset mutton I would say Blue Vinney cheese, a variety coloured by fen or blue mould and which, though difficult now to come by except in outlying farms, is considered by many to be cheese far superior to all others in the royal realm of England.

The *Dorset Echo* (16 August 2006) wrote about Dorset food when a Food Week was in the offing with a competition to find the defining Dorset dish: 'Dorset Apple Cake is proving to be a strong front-runner, with the obvious candidates of Dorset Blue Vinney and the Dorset Knob following closely behind', but fish and chips was also popular, perhaps because of its seaside associations. Apple Cake won.

The annual meeting of missionary supporters seems an unlikely setting for a posh tea, but Blanche Egerton, a daughter of the house, remembered West Stafford Rectory in the 1860s 'for days beforehand the house had been pervaded by a delicious smell of cakes and pastry cooking, and now the tired missionary supporter could do full justice to chickens, tongues and trifles. Choicest of all the luxuries, and the one which made the most impression upon our minds was a Church with Gothic windows formed of jam tartlets glued together by barley sugar, whose architect was Mrs Howe the confectioner in Dorchester.' These confections must have been fashionable. At Christmas 1859 the *Bridport News* reported in Dorchester:

HANDSOME CHRISTMAS ORNAMENT – Mr. Woolston, sugar baker, of this town, who last year fabricated so marvellously exact a model of St. Peter's Church in every detail, interior and exterior, has this season produced a superb Chinese Pagoda in white and colours, it seems to stand on a foundation of rock sugar whence spouts the crystal gush of a delicious fountain; the towering Pagoda is a most aerial and fragile but beautifully proportioned structure. A chariot with horses in tandem is driving full speed; and an elephant, directed by a sable Ethiopian, is also moving round the Pagoda – the front of which is studded with brightly coloured knobs, whose number and magnificence are supposed to be indicative of the rank and puissance of the Mandarin to whom it appertains. Two snow white flights of outer steps ascent the plateau of rock; and moving figures are seen in the courts around: stone work with its ponderous ornaments being surmounted by the open latticed shaft which, with its fantastic ornamental excesscences, throws up still another story, terminating in the glittering and gorgeously coloured cupolas, pinnacles, and fretted branches peculiar to the pagoda style, the latter protecting a series of superb bells all around the top of the structure. This effort of festive genius is entirely Mr. Woolston's own conception; and though nearly two feet in height, and in breadth well proportioned, it weighs altogether not exceeding two pounds.

THE DAILY DIET

Considering that everyone has had to eat at least once a day, and that often this meant cooked food, it is surprisingly difficult to discover the everyday food of even the recent past. From the medieval period we have some knowledge of high-class food and cooking, but little detailed information about normal eating patterns. Even in the seventeenth and eighteenth centuries, the bias is towards at least 'gentry' cooking, partly because the upper part of society was more literate, and so kept recipe books, diaries and so on; and partly because they could afford the variety of ingredients which make cookery books necessary.

Occasionally the diet of more 'ordinary' people surfaces, usually incidentally, for example if they are giving evidence for a court case. There is a little about food in the casebook Sir Francis Ashly JP Recorder of Dorchester kept, which details his examinations of witnesses. On Christmas Day 1623 three bad characters were observed in an alehouse 'having to their supper one Gannye [turkey] whose Gutts and feathers were buryed in a Clay pitt neere the said howse and covered with earth and trod down smooth'. There was also 'another great fowle whose head and legs being cutt of' the witness could not identify 'but verily thinketh that it was another Gannye'. Turkeys had been introduced form North America the century before, but they were still luxuries, unlikely to be found in an alehouse. Besides this Christmassy fare they had 'a piece of Pork boiled and the hinder part of a roasted pig cold'. About six conspirators met at the same house on New Year's Eve for a supper of 'a piece of beefe, a henne and a cople of Rabbetts', provided by themselves and cooked for them there. The conspirators were eating above their station, presumably having stolen the turkeys at least, but the emphasis on meat eating is characteristic.

John Samways of Rodden was accused in 1624 of poisoning his young wife. After they had both been out to milk the cows 'he fetched her certain raisons out of his chest, bidding her boyle them in milke'. According to the husband 'he had also had some of the raisins for his supper with her, and that after supper they had sat by the fire and ate apples roasted and put into mead'. However she fell ill, complained that the raisins were 'gristy' (gritty) and died two days later.

A domestic evening (apart from the poison) – a treat of raisins, and apples in mead by the fire – preserved for us because of the court case.

Diet is sometimes recorded because the people concerned are famous or eccentric. Henry Hastings, squire of Woodlands, came into the latter category. 'He never failed to eat oysters, both dinner and supper time, all season: the neighbouring town of Poole supplied him with them. . . . On the other side was the door of an old chapel, not used for devotion; the pulpit, as the safest place, was never wanting of a cold chine of beef, venison-pasty, gammon of bacon, or great apple-pye, with thick crust, extremely baked. His table cost him not much, though it was good to eat at. His sports supplied all but beef or mutton, except Fridays, when he had the best of salt-fish.' The description dates from 1638.

THOMAS HARDY AND T.E. LAWRENCE

Thomas Hardy's cook and parlourmaid have left accounts of his daily life in the 1910s and '20s, when he was in his seventies and eighties. For breakfast there was tea (for Hardy) or coffee (for Mrs Hardy), bacon and eggs or sometimes kippers, boiled eggs or kedgeree, and then toast and marmalade. On Sundays there were sausages. Hardy apparently sprinkled brown sugar on his bacon. Lunch was the main meal, with lamb and caper sauce a favourite. Every day Hardy had a baked custard for pudding. Tea consisted of wafer-thin bread and butter cut into small squares, and small home-made cakes. If there were no visitors, dinner was mutton broth made from scrag-end of lamb and vegetables, prepared daily, and two boiled eggs. Dorset knobs and stilton cheese finished the meal. Burgundy was served with lunch and dinner.

His parlourmaid didn't think frumenty was made at Max Gate in her time, but on the day of his death Hardy had two old-fashioned dishes made for him, at his request. Kettle-broth, made from finely chopped parsley, onions and bread cooked in hot

The 'witch' Elizabeth Endorfield preparing potatoes, with a wooden bucket for the water. From Thomas Hardy's Under the Greenwood Tree, *first illustrated edition, 1878.*

water, was traditional invalid food for him, and a rasher of bacon was cooked on his bedroom fire. Both of these are cottage dishes, prepared without an oven. They must have been familiar to him from his childhood at Bockhampton.

Hardy was not seen as a lavish housekeeper, but T.E. Lawrence was worse. At least there was cooking done at Max Gate: Lawrence thought Cloud's Hill too small to cook in, and kept 'bread, butter and cheese under glass bells and [went] out occasionally to spend a few pennies on bacon and eggs or fish and chips; to one who ate only when hungry the plainest fare was more desirable than the strange mixtures of ingenious chefs'. The glass domes are still there. On Christmas day 1932 Lawrence recorded that he and an airman staying at Cloud's Hill 'walked for fourteen miles and dinnered off a tinned chicken. The long walk made it taste good.' This was high living for Cloud's Hill: a colleague at Bovington remembered his groceries being delivered to the station: '100lb jars of jam (assorted), 2lbs each of several varieties of cheese, 50 bottles of fruit salad, 50 tins of "Ideal" milk, etc.'

COOKING METHODS

It is easy to see the cooking of earlier times as unsophisticated, to imagine medieval feasts as roast meat, ale and bread, but the reality was different. Even in medieval times a great variety of imported spices, dried fruits, nuts and lemons were available to flavour food. When this was added to native products complex recipes were possible, and were used by those rich enough to afford them. The medieval peasant's everyday fare was probably only bread, cheese and the vegetables and herbs he grew or gathered himself, but anyone above that level would have had much more variety. Ginger, cinnamon, cardamom, nutmeg, cloves, saffron, sandalwood and pepper were used for both meat and sweet dishes. Lists of dishes at feasts, and medieval recipe books, record elaborate meals, with, for example, beef olives – thin slices of beef with spicy stuffing – chicken stuffed with garlic and grapes, fish in wine sauce. Sugar was little used, being regarded as an expensive spice; honey was used for sweetening and potatoes were unknown, but a great variety of vegetables were grown including peas, beans, carrots, cabbage, lettuces, leeks and onions. Wild herbs were used for soups and salads, and a great variety of wild birds was eaten, including swans (the swans at Abbotsbury were not originally for ornament). Many smaller birds like the hundreds of wheatears trapped annually on Portland were relished, and dovecotes produced a handy supply of young birds.

The small household of Munden's Chantry, Bridport, shows how the middle classes lived. Their mid-fifteenth century account book shows that everyday purchases were bread, beer, meat, fish, and milk products, but saffron, mustard, vinegar, pepper, cloves, ginger and cinnamon were bought to spice the food, and imports such as figs, almonds, raisins and dates added variety.

Tea, coffee and chocolate were all unknown, so hot drinks would be spiced wine or mulled ale, mead or herb infusions. Beer, ale made with hops, was not made until the sixteenth century. Gradually new ingredients were imported, many of which were found to grow happily in this country, like the potato. Additions go on being made: kiwi fruit, avocados, aubergines and even courgettes are all very recent introductions.

The cooking methods of the past seem to us awkward and difficult to control, so we expect the cookery to be crude. This is not true; cooking over an open fire is very adaptable, but we have lost the skills needed, and forget the great variety of utensils and devices which evolved for cooking over them.

Boiling is the easiest method on an open fire: a large cauldron of boiling water will steadily cook a whole meal, with a meat pudding and a sweet one, in cloths, and vegetables in nets to keep them separate. Joints of meat were boiled without covering, but the pot needed a lid to keep soot or anything else falling down the chimney from joining the dinner. Porridge (or Hasty Pudding as it was called in the eighteenth century) was cooked in a smaller pan over the fire as were many dishes.

Saucepans with legs stood in the fire, and legless ones were either suspended from a chain, or stood on a trivet. It is possible to bake with an open fire too, by heating a large metal pot over the fire and inverting it over the bread, pie or whatever which was placed on a metal sheet. The heat radiating from the pot cooked the food. If long cooking was needed hot embers were put around and on the pot. The difficulty is telling how the food is cooking, since lifting up the pot disperses a lot of the heat. Some open hearths had the fire raised on a metal plate supported by bricks, so that the space beneath could be used as an oven. Girdles, flat iron plates with a handle for suspension, seem not to have been used in the south until about 1800, although they were in common in the north long before, and were used, greased, for cooking barley cakes, scones and biscuits.

Even in the eighteenth century meat was not roasted in the oven, but by the ancient method on a spit in front of the open fire. From the early nineteenth century shiny screens called hasteners were used behind the meat to reflect the heat and speed cooking.

Ovens have been used since the Iron Age, and were common in larger medieval houses and bakeries. By the eighteenth century they were found in farmhouses and the better cottages. The ovens were brick or stone structures, usually built to one side of the fireplace. They were domed, with usually an iron door (see Bread for a description of using these ovens). They took a long time to cool down, so a succession of dishes could be cooked after the bread: pastry, then cakes, and finally stews.

Ranges, cast-iron stoves with ovens beside the fire, were developed from the mid-eighteenth century, and used coal as fuel rather than wood. At first the fire was open, but from the early nineteenth century versions were available with an enclosed fire and a hotplate. At first ranges were confined to the rich, as they were expensive. Thomas Weld of Lulworth Castle bought one in London in 1790, and it cost £23 without fitting. During the nineteenth century ranges were installed in many farmhouses and cottages, but cooking over an open fire did not die out completely until the twentieth century.

Ranges were an improvement, but required a lot of managing. The heat in the oven tended to be one-sided, and wind direction could have a bad effect. From about 1890 gas, and from the 1920s electricity, started to replace coal-fired ranges, although there are still many Agas (invented in 1929) and other developed ranges to be found in use.

Complaints about the state of modern cooking are constant: everyone sees the food of their youth, or even the food of a past they can't remember, as ambrosial. Ralph Wightman in 1947 complained of 'the decay in good housekeeping':

Even in my lifetime almost everything eaten in a farmhouse was prepared and preserved at home. The war has cut off supplies and driven a few country wives to look up the recipes of their grandmothers, but I am afraid that peace will see them slipping back again. It will be too easy to buy bread from the baker, bacon from the stores, butter and cheese from New Zealand, beer from the brewery, tinned fruit from the ends of the earth, preserves, pickles, sauces, soups, meats, even vegetables in tins and bottles. It is a great pity, because it means that a couple of generations have grown up who have never known the taste of first-class food and drink. The

E. BROWN & SON'S PRIZE KITCHEN RANGE, OF WHICH UPWARDS OF 4000, HAVE BEEN SOLD. Full particulars, Testimonials, &c. may be obtained on application, and Ranges seen in operation at the Works, Broad Street, Lyme Regis. KITCHEN RANGES AND REGISTER STOVES OF EVERY DESCRIPTION.

Iron ranges were manufactured in Dorset – Brown's of Lyme Regis produced several sizes. This is from an advertisement of 1857.

factories make good standard articles, they never turn out anything as bad as a home-made failure, but they never approach the perfection of a home-made success.

I suppose it is partly the appalling bad home products which have driven us all to the standard factory article. When I was a boy every farmhouse cured its own bacon at home. The best of it was better than anything ever sold in a shop, but the worst was rancid and almost uneatable.

Dorset food is always changing. Fashion, new ingredients, new equipment or methods all contribute to the changes. Drinking habits are a good demonstration of this. From the medieval period ale or beer was the staple drink, taken even for breakfast. During the seventeenth century, tea, coffee and chocolate started to be imported. At first they were luxuries, but by the middle of the nineteenth century even the labourers of Dorset regarded tea as their main drink, or even worse a substitute made by soaking burnt toast in boiling water. (*In Far from the Madding Crowd* 'a boiling pipkin of charred bread called "coffee"' sat by the fire in Warren's Malthouse.) The beer had been a valuable addition to their diet: tea was not, particularly as it was mostly drunk without milk.

The Recipes Here
The recipes in this book are mostly taken from eleven surviving manuscript recipe books which are described in the bibliography, supplemented with recollections and material from many sources. Recipes using Dorset raw materials have been preferred.

METRIC CONVERSION TABLES

Imperial	Metric
16oz (1lb)	450g
8oz (½lb)	225g
4oz (¼lb)	100g
1oz	25g

Metric

1,000 gram (g) = 1 kilogram (kilo)

Metric	Imperial
1 kilo (1000 g)	2lb 3oz
½ kilo (500 g)	1lb 2oz
¼ kilo (250 g)	9oz
100 g	4oz

Harvesting oats with a reaper-binder in 1936, probably at Evershot.

NOTE FOR YEAST RECIPES

There are basically three sorts of yeast in use today. Fresh yeast can be bought in health food shops and some bakeries, and dried yeasts, either in proprietory packets, or loose from health food shops. Loose dried yeast, some packeted sorts, and fresh yeast need to be 'started' before being added to the flour. This means that they have to be put into about ¼ pint of warm water with a teaspoonful of sugar. After about 20 minutes the mixture should be bubbling slightly, and is ready to use.

Some proprietory dried yeasts do not need 'starting' and are simply mixed with the flour. Read the packet to be sure which sort you have. I have found all three sorts satisfactory. Fresh yeast is cheapest, but will only keep for a week.

Coming back from milking near Bridport in the 1890s. The man on the left carries big cans of milk supported on a yoke across his shoulders. (Bridport Museum)

DOMESTIC OVEN TEMPERATURES

	Electric (°F)	Celsius (°C)	Gas
Very hot	450	230	8
Hot	425	220	7
Fairly hot	400	200	6
Fairly hot	375	190	5
Moderate	350	180	4
Warm	325	170	3
Cool	300	150	2
Cool	275	140	1
Very cool	250	130	½
Very cool	225	110	¼

LIQUID MEASURES
(approximate equivalents)
Metric
1 litre = 10 decilitres (dl) = 100 centilitres (cl) = 1000 millilitres (ml)

Imperial	Metric
1 quart	1.1 litres
1 pint	6 dl
½ pint	3 dl
¼ pint	1.5 dl
1 tablespoon	15 ml
1 dessertspoon	10 ml
1 teaspoon	5 ml

Metric	Imperial
1 litre	35 fluid oz
½ litre (5 dl)	18 fluid oz
¼ litre (2.5 dl)	9 fluid oz
1 dl	4 fluid oz

Dorset watercress. (Jesty collection)

Acknowledgements

Many people have helped with this book: I am very grateful to them. As always, the staffs of the Dorset County Library (lending and reference) and the Dorset Record Office have been friendly supports. Mr T.W. Jesty has kindly told me about watercress, and lent photographs. In Dorchester, Andrew Holland, butcher, and Mary and David Nesling of Down to Earth have discussed recipes with me, and helped with ingredients. David Winship of Moore's Bakery, Morcombelake, told me about Dorset knobs, and Norman Smith of Weymouth Bakeries gave me a recipe for dough cake. Lyme Regis and Bridport Museums, the Jesty family, and Moore's Bakery have kindly allowed the use of photographs. Margaret Holmes; Polly and Michael Legg; Alan Roberts of the National Farmers' Union; Dr George Tee; and Dr Sadie Ward of the Museum of English Rural Life, Reading, have all discussed recipes and sources with me. Dr Bernard Jones kindly nailed down a quotation from William Barnes. We are also grateful to those copyright holders not individually acknowledged, and apologise to those with whom it has proved impossible to make contact. Major General H.M.G. Bond very kindly lent me the Tyneham manuscript cookery book from which so many of these recipes come. Sheena Pearce has again managed to decipher my untidy manuscript. My mother helped in many ways, with the text and with the cooking, and Christopher has eaten everything.

This revised edition includes recipes from the Sadborow book generously given to me by Jenny Roger. George Tee kindly sent me Dorset recipes from Mary Byron's *Pot Luck* (1927) and Patricia Vale sent the Devonshire Buildings, Weymouth's version of Mother Eve's Pudding. All illustrations are from the author's collection unless otherwise stated.

Transporting watercress directly from the beds at Doddings, Bere Regis. (Jesty collection)

Soup

Watercress pickers at Waterstone, late 1930s. (Jesty collection)

Soup

Soups abound in eighteenth-century recipe books, although some of them are closer to stews. There are four different recipes for white soup in the Tyneham recipe book alone. Pease soup is the other popular one, and both are known from the medieval period.

Almond Soup

WHITE SOUP
Take a Nuckle of Veal with a Blade or two of Mace and an Oynion stuck with cloves A little whole peper a bit of lean Bacon boyl it very well, when half boy'ld take a lean large fowl half roasted beat all to pieces like a past, a little lemon peel, when it is thoroughly boyl'd take half a pd of Almonds blanch'd and let it boil a little while longer Add a little more cream according to yr whiteness you like it, Salt to your tast, then strain it thro, a sive first and then thro' a jelly Bag if you have mind you may put in Rise when boil'd or vermijelly – then heat it up with little toasted Manchets and a roasted Chick in the middle if you please – If you have no Almonds a few [bay] leaves will give the Almond tast.

3oz almonds	chopped-up cooked chicken
1½ pints of chicken stock, made with mace, cloves and lemon peel	vermicelli or small soup pasta
	cream (optional)

This can be made either as a soup or a complete supper dish. Blanch the almonds and remove their skins. Liquidise with some of the stock, leaving some crunchy bits. (If you haven't a liquidiser, use ground almonds.) Add to the rest of the stock and bring to the boil with the chopped chicken. Simmer for 15 minutes, and then add the vermicelli or soup pasta and cream if used. Continue simmering until the pasta is done.

This has an unusual fresh taste, somehow more like new hazelnuts than almonds. The almonds are crunchy, and it seems silly to remove them as this Tyneham recipe does. With 4oz vermicelli this makes a filling dish for two or three, or with a couple of ounces of pasta (and without the chicken) a good soup for four.

Mrs Clavel's White Soup

Another interesting white soup from Tyneham is a recipe supplied by Mrs Clavel, presumably of Smedmore House, Kimmeridge, just to the east of Tyneham.

TO MAKE WHITE SOUP, MRS CLAVEL
Take a Fowl or Knuckle of Veal put it into a Gallon of Water and boil it two hours put in a blade of Mace and a clove or two, then Strain it off and skim of the fat, then boil it for half an hour and put in a quarter of an oz of Vermicelli take half a pint of

cream and a spoonful of flower and mix it together – serve it up with a French Roll and you may add if you like it a few Leeks or Spinage.

This is a thin soup, and very adaptable. Chicken stock today is more likely to be made from the carcass of a roast chicken.

about 1½ pints chicken stock	1lb leeks, chopped
cooked chicken, cut into smallish pieces	4oz vermicelli

The chicken stock should be prepared by boiling the bones, skin, etc. from a roast chicken, along with the jelly which forms under the fat removed from the roasting, a blade of mace, two cloves, salt and any clean vegetable peelings about. Boil for 20 minutes: the 2 hours suggested by Mrs Clavel is not necessary since one is not cooking a whole bird. Strain, allow to cool and take the fat off the top. The spices add a delicate and unusual flavour to the stock.

Heat up the stock with the chicken pieces in, boil for 5 minutes, then add the chopped leeks. Simmer for a couple of minutes, then add the vermicelli and boil for another couple of minutes. Serve.

This makes a complete meal, which tastes as Mrs Clavel intended but with a lot more leek and vermicelli. A little cream could be added. Very quick to make once the stock is done, and very adaptable. Adding only a little vermicelli or one of the tiny soup pastas, a finely chopped leek and omitting the chicken pieces would make a fine soup. Spinach seems a bit strong to add to chicken stock. Rice would be a good alternative to vermicelli, but would need longer cooking.

Green Pease Soup (Summer)

Pease soup occurs in all the recipe books, sometimes with onions or meat. Tyneham has several, all of which should be made with good stock. It is the unusual flavouring of these stocks which give the soups their character. In the mid-seventeenth century Sir Kenelme Digby was right about this as so much else in cooking: 'The ground or body of Potages [soups] must always be very good broth.' The good broth should be made by boiling the spices specified in the recipe with bones, clean vegetable (or even fruit) peelings and salt and pepper for about 20 minutes. Then strain, allow to cool and remove the fat from the top.

TO MAKE GREEN PEASE SOUP

Take a large knuckle of veal put a peck of Pease shells and a large handful of Onions well cover'd with Water, if your veal is not large you must add a scrag of mutton, let it stew till it is quite to pieces, then strain it of, and put to it a peck of fresh Pease and a few Spring Carrots, green it with the juice of Spinach and Season it to your tast – you may add a Cabbage lettice cut, with a Cucumber Sliced.

2 pints stock, made with pea shells and spring onions about ½lb carrots, chopped	about 2lb peas (before shelling) about ¼lb spinach lettuce (optional)

Bring the strained stock to the boil with the chopped carrots and boil for about 5 minutes. Add the shelled peas, boil for about 3 to 4 minutes, add the finely chopped spinach and boil for a minute or two until that is cooked.

All the quantities are fairly arbitrary: this is a June soup, designed to use young vegetables. The spring onions could be used well chopped in the final soup rather than the stock, and lettuce could be added a minute or so before serving.

Green Pease Soup (Winter)

Take 3; 4; or 5 pd of lean beef with 3 pints of pease into 2 Gallons of Water, let it boyl till the Meat is all to Raggs, and half an hour before you strain it off put in two or 3 Anchovys and an Onion Stuck with Cloves a Race of ginger bruis'd, a Faggot of Thyme Savory and parsley and some pepper then strain it and let it Boyl with a little Mint and Salt to your Tast, then add burnt Butter some forced Meat Balls and bits of bacon bread cut in dice and fryed Crisp Spinage boyl'd Green, Roots of Sallery boyl'd in it and so serve it up.

3 pints stock, made with cloves, ginger and herbs as above, or with just the spices ½lb of dried peas, soaked overnight	½lb bacon pieces ½lb onion, chopped flour (optional)

Boil the peas in the stock until cooked, about 40 minutes. Fry the bacon pieces and the chopped onion, strain the fat off and add to the soup, or add 1 to 1½oz flour to the bacon, onion and fat, stir to make a roux, then steadily add the stock. Combine and heat through.

A very substantial peasant dish, strongly flavoured, with the rather bland peas cheered up by the spices in the stock. If thickened it is nearly solid. Best with a strong green vegetable like sprouting broccoli, or spinach.

Celery Soup

Sorrel is used in one early eighteenth-century recipe for pease soup, to improve the flavour, and celery in a later eighteenth-century one. Celery is also found in another soup at Tyneham.

SELLERY SOUP

Take a leg of veal and boil with 2 ounces of rice 3 blades of Mace and a bounch green Sellery, Cover it with water, 6 or 7 quarts, when half done Slice in Sellery roots and stew it, till all the goodness of the Meat is out, salt it to your Tast, and fry bread Crisp in Butter, to serve up with it, garnish with what you like

1 pint stock	1 tablespoon long grain rice
good pinch of mace	vermicelli (optional)
about 4 lengths celery	

Bring all the ingredients to the boil, and simmer until the rice is cooked, about 10–15 minutes. Alternatively simmer the stock, celery and mace for 5–10 minutes, then add a couple of ounces of vermicelli, cook for a minute or two until done. This makes a more substantial soup: adding a larger quantity of rice would have the same effect, but the stock would need diluting a little. Some small pieces of cooked chicken would be a good addition, and make it into a complete supper. Celery and mace work well together, an unusual combination. A pinch of mace added to any celery soup recipe would be good.

Inside Bridport and District Co-operative Society in the 1920s, with beautifully arranged tins and packets (some with soup): a long way from the farm photographs. (Bridport Museum)

Packing watercress, c. 1910. The willow baskets were called flats, and were returned empty for re-use. (Jesty collection)

Watercress Soup

small onion	bunch of watercress
1½oz butter or margarine	1oz flour
½ pint chicken stock (from a cube or home-made)	

Chop the onion and fry in the fat. Add the stock, then put the contents of the frying pan, the top (leafy) half of the bunch of watercress, and the flour in a liquidiser. Render as fine or coarse as you wish, then cook it for 5 minutes in a saucepan (the stemmy bits of the watercress left from this recipe make a good addition to the stock-pot). Cream may be added, if desired, and nutmeg makes an unusual flavouring.

This makes a good soup very quickly: two people can easily eat this amount, so multiply as necessary. If you don't have a liquidiser cook the onion in a saucepan, add the flour and make a roux, add the stock and chopped-up watercress, then cook for 5 minutes.

The addition of potatoes (say ½lb) cooked in the stock and mashed or liquidised make a different but equally good soup.

Fish

The small eate sweete, the great more daintily
The great will seeth or bake, the small will frye.
For rich mens tables serve the greater fish.
The small are to the poor a daintie dish.

THOMAS BASTARD, *1598, vicar of Bere Regis*

Seine netting, probably at Charmouth, 1912. (Lyme Regis Museum)

Fish

With its long, varied coastline and rivers, Dorset has always had fish in quantity and of great variety. Some species have disappeared through over-fishing or natural changes. Up to the sixteenth century pilchards were caught from Weymouth and exported to Spain. Oysters were a cheap food, popular with the poor, until the mid-nineteenth century, when over-fishing and perhaps pollution reduced their numbers.

In the 1790s Daniel Defoe visited Poole, 'famous for the best and biggest oysters in all this part of England, which the people of Pool pretend to be famous for pickling, and they are barrelled up here, and sent not only to London, but to the West Indies, and to Spain, and Italy, and other parts. 'Tis observed more pearl are found in the Pool oysters, and larger than in any other oysters about England.' Oysters were found around Tyneham, and are a common garnish for fish dishes in recipes from there.

Hutchins, the county historian, emphasised the variety available in the later eighteenth century: 'The sea on our coasts abound with Stugeon, Turbot, Mackarel, Plaice, Soles, Basse, Whitings, Congers, Porpoises, Lobsters, red and grey Mullet, Thornback, Piper or Gurnet, Frill or Scollop, Shrimps, Prawns and Oysters. Our rivers furnish Salmon, Eels, Trout, Pike, Carp, Gudgeon, Tench and Perch. . . . The only considerable FISHERY is that of mackerel. . . . Between Lyme and Portland they are caught in great numbers from April to June, and furnish the London markets. They are good provision for the poor, who split, dry and salt them for winter use.'

Daniel Defoe saw the fishing between Abbotsbury and Bridport in the 1720s. The mackerel 'they take in the easiest way imaginable! For they fix one end of the net to a pole set deep into the sand, then the net being in a boat, they row right out into the water some length, then turn and row parallel with the shore veering out the net all the while until they have let go all the net, except the line at the end and then the boat rows on shore, when the men hauling the net to the shore at both ends bring to shore such fish, as they surrounded in the little way they rowed, this at that time proved to be an incredible number in so much that the men could hardly draw them on shore.'

In 1905 the *Victoria County History* found just the same method being used, except there was no pole 'as there are generally enough loafers on the shore to hold one end of the rope attached to the seine'. In 1905 look-outs were posted, as they had been for centuries, to watch for the shoals. 'Usually the crew are waiting in a neighbouring public-house, or in a convenient cottage with a hogshead of cider. Report states that three hogsheads have been consumed by men waiting for long-delayed fish. . . . As Dorset cider is a quarrelsome drink, its consumption leads to rough language and rougher behaviour. Sometimes when two crews crossed their seines in pursuit of the same school of fish they "larrupped" one another with their tongues while their friends on the beach assisted in the quarrel with pebbles.'

Mackerel shoals started appearing in March, and at Tyneham when the weekly Bible reading in church got round to the story of Balaam and Balak (showing the right date had arrived), all the fishermen would ceremonially leave the church to look for a shoal.

The *Bridport News* reported extraordinary catches in June 1873. The fishing had been good all week, with one boat from Burton Bradstock bringing in 6,000 fish, but then another brought in 16,300 mackerel in one haul and these huge catches continued. 'The fish met with a ready sale. . . . When the boat-loads arrived, the crowds of people who gathered upon the beach vied with each other in their business capabilities . . . the bulk of the fish was packed and carted, to be taken to the railway station without loss of time.' On the beach very large fish made 10*s* a hundred or 8*s* a hundred for smaller ones on Monday, but by Tuesday the price had fallen to 2*s* 6*d* per hundred.

This inshore mackerel fishery has largely gone, destroyed, the old fishermen think, by the large ships which work further out, scooping up the fish before they get close to the shore.

Herring were less important in Dorset, but they were caught, and at Swanage 'in the year 1788, William Morton Pitt, esq., set on foot a plan for the establishment of a herring fishery, and manufactory of dried herrings. . . . Several houses were erected for smoking and curing them; and it is generally allowed the fish taken and cured here are equal to those procured from any other part of the kingdom.' The manufactory was producing red herrings, not kippers, since the kipper was not

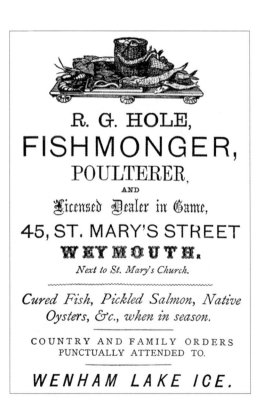

An 1874 advertisement for a Weymouth fishmonger. They often sold ice.

invented until about 1850. Red herrings were heavily salted and smoked, ending up hard, salty and red from the smoke.

Mackerel with Gooseberry Sauce

Mackerel should be very fresh, and are then good rolled in oatmeal and fried or grilled. Gooseberry or fennel sauces are traditional, and do improve the fish.

About ½lb gooseberries	knob of butter
4 mackerel, gutted and headless	

Top and tail the gooseberries and put a few of them, sliced, in the gutted fish. Wrap the fish in foil and bake at gas mark 5 until the fish are cooked, probably about 20 minutes. Cook the rest of the gooseberries in a saucepan with just enough water to cover them. When soft mash with a good knob of butter and serve with the fish.

A pinch of ginger can be added to the sauce and, if the gooseberries are awfully sharp, a little sugar.

Mackerel with Fennel Sauce

The fish can be cooked with leaves from either the herb fennel, or Florence fennel, the vegetable. A sprinkling of nutmeg goes well with it.

FENNEL SAUCE	
1oz butter	2 tablespoons chopped fennel
1oz flour	a good pinch of nutmeg (optional)
½ pint milk, water or fish stock	

Heat the butter in a good thick saucepan, add the flour and mix together thoroughly. Slowly add the liquid so that it thickens. Simmer for 5 minutes, then add the chopped fennel (and nutmeg) and continue simmering for another 5 minutes.

No matter which liquid is used, it must be thoroughly cooked or it will taste floury. I think fish stock is best, although the fennel is so strong that water does work. Milk is perhaps a little rich for such an oily fish.

Mackerel in Cider

A simpler way with mackerel is to bake them in foil as above with slices of lemon inside, and then squeeze more lemon over them when cooked. They can also be baked in cider, needing about 20 minutes in the oven at gas mark 7.

*Mackerel fishing at Abbotsbury, c. 1910.
The man with the bowler hat is Bill Ferry,
the owner of one of the boats, and the
others are his crew with visitors.*

Tyneham Sauce

Instructions for cooking most types of fish are not found in the manuscript cookery books, presumably because they were simply fried or baked. However there are several sauces for serving with fish.

WHITE FISH SAUCE (TYNEHAM)
An anchovy a bit of Onion a Little whole pepper Boil'd up pretty strong with water then Strain it off and melt your butter up with it Shrimps or oysters add to it with sliced Lemons.

about 4oz onion, sliced and fried	6 peppercorns
3 strips of anchovies	¾ pint water

Bring all ingredients to the boil and simmer for 5 minutes. Liquidise and reheat. If you haven't a liquidiser, chop the onion finely and grind the pepper before using.

This is a good fish sauce, which goes well with white fish such as cod. Oysters are an unlikely addition today, and shrimps would be too delicate for the sauce. Squeezed lemon adds piquancy.

White Fish in Sauce

A rather similar sauce from Blandford, from about 1810, is used to poach the fish:

To Stew Flounders, Plaice or Soals
Half fry your Fish and take not quite a quarter of a pound of butter and brown it, put to it a quart of water 2 anchovies and one onion boil this Liquor slowly a quarter of an hour then put your fish with some shrimps and stew them 20 minutes then take out the Fish and put in a spoonful of vinegar and give it one boil up put a little Flour and Butter to thicken the Sauce if you put in any oysters or Cockles Liquor it must be very little before you take it off the fire.

an onion	dash of vinegar
2 or 3 strips of anchovy	1½oz butter and flour (optional)
1–1½lb whole plaice, flounders or sole, beheaded and gutted	

Chop the onion finely, and bring to the boil in about ¾ pint of water with the anchovy strips. Put the fish in an ovenproof dish and pour the sauce over, adding the dash of vinegar. Bake in the oven at gas mark 5 for about 20 minutes. If you want the sauce to be thick, when the fish are done remove them from the sauce, and thicken the sauce with the flour and butter, cooking it through for 5 minutes.

Slightly less spicy than the previous sauce, and good for poaching white fish.

Sole and Turbot

These two fine flatfish have been caught off the Dorset coast for centuries. Neither occurs in the early cookery books, probably because they need only very simple cooking to be perfect.

Sole should be skinned, grilled for only about 5 minutes a side, and served with butter in which parsley and lemon has been mixed. The happy association of fish and parsley dates from at least the medieval period.

Turbot are larger, and it is better to bake them in the oven, wrapped in foil for about 20 minutes to the pound at gas mark 4.

Spicy Sprats (or Herring)

To bake sprats take an equal quantity of allspice, pepper, mace and cloves and nutmeg beat them together and put in a little salt, then take your sprats washed and guted and lay them in a pan and between every layer of sprats sprinkle a little spice

Fish seller at Bridport, 1890s.

then fill with liquor made of white wine and vinegar and a little water and cover them with a double paper and put them in the oven.

Mrs Machen's recipe is very simple, but very spicy. Cider or fish stock could be used instead of wine.

1½lb of sprats, gutted and headless (herring are also good)
¾ teaspoon each ground allspice, pepper, mace, cloves and nutmeg

about ⅓ pint vinegar wine
about ⅓ pint cider, fish stock or white wine

Put layers of sprats interspersed with layers of spice in an ovenproof dish with a lid. Fill with the liquid and bake at gas mark 7 for about 20 minutes.

Herring in Beer

Herrings are best simply rolled in beaten egg and oatmeal and fried, served with wedges of lemon. Tyneham has one sauce:

HERRING SAUCE
Take the Heads fry ym in a pan a little, then boil them in Stale Beer with a bit of onion and a little whole pepper Strain it off, then Melt your butter in it and boyl it up till thick.

Presumably this is a sauce to serve with herrings, but it could be used to cook them in. Fresh beer would be fine!

Marinated Herring

Loose in Mrs Machen's cookery book is a recipe for spiced herrings rather like that for sprats:

TO MARRINATE HERRINGS
Take the largest of Herring and Cut off their Heds and tails then wash them Gut them and dry them with a Cloth put them in an earthen pan with bay leaves between each lay half a pint of salt and half an ounce of Pepper and the same Quantity of Nutmegs beaten fine and strew'd on them Pour in Vinegar Cover with a flannel paste them over and bak them over with Brown bread.

I think the last bit means cover with a flannel and then pastry and bake at the same temperature as brown bread. The coverings are simply a lid and would have been discarded. The half a pint of salt may be a mistake for half an ounce, unless the recipe was intended to preserve the herrings.

4 herring, gutted and beheaded	6 bay leaves
¾ teaspoon each of ground nutmeg and pepper	about ½ pint white wine vinegar

Put the herring in a baking dish with a lid, interspersed with the spices and bay leaves. Pour on the vinegar and water to cover, and bake at gas mark 4 for about 25 minutes.

Lobster Pie

Lobsters used to be cheap: when John O'Keefe stayed at Lulworth in 1791 he ate them all the time, and was amazed to find that the pots were baited with puffins taken from the cliffs. In 1751 the household accounts from Loders show two lobsters for 7½d the pair, while in the same week a dozen mackerel cost 6d, a pound of butter 4¼d and a shoulder of mutton 1s 6d.

This 1709 Bloxworth recipe may not be cheap, but is possible:

Advertising lobster teas at the Picnic Inn, Osmington, 1930s.

Take your lobster when boyled and spleet the taile in 2 or 3 pieces and the claws season it with peper salt nutmeg put in your pasty and cover it with butter then take the body of your lobsters and the seed of your hen lobsters and beat them in a mortar with a little strong broth or oyster Liqor and some butter put it into your pye.

Part of the lobster meat is being used in chunks, and the rest pounded with liquid and butter to make a sauce to put in the pasty to keep it moist.

Crab Tart

In the 1690s Celia Fiennes visited Tyneham: 'there I eate the best lobsters and crabs being boyled in the sea water and scarce cold, very large and sweet'. Crabs are still easily bought along the Dorset coast, and are best cooked in very salty water: about 1½oz salt to each pint of water. The hard work comes with extracting the meat from the body and legs. Good-quality ready-extracted meat saves all that. Crab is good simply with a salad but, since it has a strong taste, it is also good cooked with other things.

Pastry	*Filling*
6oz plain flour	tablespoon lemon juice
3oz butter	teaspoon Worcestershire sauce
pinch each of salt and cayenne pepper	½–¾lb crab meat
cold water to mix	⅛ pint (4fl oz) double cream
3 eggs	

Rub the flour and butter together thoroughly, add the salt and cayenne and enough water just to make a paste. Rest the pastry in the fridge for half an hour. Roll out and line a 9-inch flan dish (it should be at least a couple of inches deep). Prick the bottom and bake at gas mark 6 for about 10 minutes. Beat the eggs lightly with the lemon juice, and Worcestershire sauce, stir in the crab meat and then the cream. Pour into the pastry case, and bake for gas mark 5 for about half an hour.

Can be eaten hot or cold. A few chopped spring onions are a good addition.

Crab Cheesecake

Filling	*Pastry*
8oz curd cheese	6oz plain flour
4oz butter or margarine	3oz butter or 2½oz margarine
tablespoon lemon juice	pinch of salt
2 egg yolks	
8oz crab meat	

An entry for Dorchester carnival in the 1930s – Jack Durnford's fish delivery van with a clear message.

Rub the flour, pinch of salt and butter together thoroughly, and add just enough cold water to make a paste. Rest the pastry in the fridge for half an hour. Line an 8- or 9-inch dish (at least a couple of inches deep), prick the bottom with a fork and bake at gas mark 5–6 for 10 minutes. Put the curd cheese, butter or margarine, lemon juice and egg yolks in a bowl and mix thoroughly. Fold in the crab meat. Bake at gas mark 4 for 35 to 45 minutes.

Very filling. The cheese and crab are good together, and the recipe would make good small tarts.

Dorset Stewed Eels

TO STEW EELS, MRS GUTHRIE

Boyle them in a great deal of water and through away that water and put ym in a little water and let ym stew tell they are enuff done with a bunch of harbes and horse radish and what other seasoning you pleas then thicken up with butter and Raspings of white bread.

From Mrs Machen. Breadcrumbs were the medieval thickening for sauces.

½–¾lb skinned eel, cut into 3-inch chunks	About 6 peppercorns, a little horse radish, a bay leaf, a little thyme and
1oz butter	marjoram (or a selection of those) about 4oz white breadcrumbs

Lightly cook the eel in the butter, in the pan they will be stewed in. Then add the herbs, peppercorns, and horseradish, and enough water to cover the eel. Bring slowly to the boil and simmer for 45 minutes. Strain, preserving the eel and the cooking water. Return these to the pan and reheat, slowly adding the breadcrumbs until it is thick enough. When it has come to the boil, serve.

At Tyneham eels were roasted stuffed with suet, herbs, shallots, pepper and nutmeg and fried with breadcrumbs, lemon peel, thyme and marjoram.

Carp

Carp were treated even more elaborately than eels at Tyneham:

TO STEW CARP WHITE
Stew them in White Wine Cider and water put in a bunch of sweet Herbs some Lemon peel Anchovie a little Mace Cloves and Nutmeg a Shallot, when the fish is done take it out and boil the Liquor a little while, thicken it with the Butter and some gravy, garnish with horse radish barbys and lemon sippets fryd Crisp and likewise the Rows fry'd, put in a spoonful of cream after the butter is in.

Lemon, anchovy, spice, shallots, horseradish and barberries all together seems rather like throwing the store cupboard at the poor fish. Another recipe from Tyneham has them rubbed with salt, stewed in red wine with an onion stuck with cloves, nutmeg, mace, lemon peel, pepper, a bundle of thyme and sweet marjoram and two anchovies. The liquor was thickened with egg yolks, butter and enriched with catchup (or ketchup), lemon juice, mushrooms, grated brown bread, and the whole garnished with lemon, barberries and horseradish!

Salmon

Salmon are taken from several Dorset rivers, but Christchurch is the most famous salmon fishery to this day.

C.J. Cornish visited the fishery in the 1890s, and his *Wild England of Today* (1895) described 'the most ancient and primitive' fishery. In the short channel through which the harbour waters pour into the sea the net-fishing goes on without ceasing from the beginning of the ebb till the turn of the tide. The order of fishing is settled by agreement, and each boat in turn is rowed out into the stream carrying the far end of the net, while the other is held upon the shore by a partner, who walks opposite as boat and net are swung down by the stream. Before the mouth is reached the boat completes its circle, and comes to shore, where both ends of the net are made fast. Then comes the hauling of the net. Both men pull the wet mass rapidly in hand-over-hand, pausing now and again to fling out masses of sea-weed, until the last twenty yards of the net are reached. If the bosom cork is ducking under, if the gently bellying folds of the long-meshed tough are in a tumult, there is one salmon or more in the net, enough to repay the fishers for a score of fruitless casts.'

At Bloxworth in 1767: 'Paid for two salmon at Ten pence pound £1.6.3.' They must have weighed about 15lb each, and were costing three times as much per pound as beef.

Poached Salmon

Cooking a whole fish means having a container big enough to heat it in, a fish kettle. The fish should be gutted, and the gills removed. The liquid should be water, with a little wine vinegar, a pinch of salt and a few peppercorns. For serving hot, bring to the boil and just simmer for 10 minutes to the pound and 10 minutes over. If it is to be served cold it is enough to simmer for 10 minutes, and then allow to cool slowly. Conventionally the backbone is removed before serving and the fish reassembled, as this makes serving easier.

Baked Salmon

This is better for cutlets. Wrap each cutlet in foil along with a squeeze of lemon juice and about an ounce of butter. Place on a metal tray and cook in the oven at gas mark 5 for 15–20 minutes. Small or chopped mushrooms can be included with them.

Red Mullet

Weymouth boasted in 1791 of 'the choicest Fish from the west every day that the wind will permit, exclusive of what are caught in its environs; and consist of Red Mullets, John Dories, Soals, Cod, Turbot, Pipers, Gurnets, Mackarel, herrings, Lobsters, Crabs, and Prawns'. The variety was appreciated by the aristocratic visitors to Weymouth from the later eighteenth century, and the guide book continues, describing the fishermen as if they had been arranged as a tourist attraction:

whilst the fishermen are engaged in the avocations, upon hauling the Seyne, bring to shore extraordinary productions of the ocean, well worthy of inspection, and highly entertaining to the curious.

The late Duke of Portland was in the habit of going to Weymouth during the summer months for the sake of the red mullet which formerly abounded there. The largest used to be had for threepence or fourpence a piece, but he has been known to give two guineas for one weighing a pound and a half. His Grace's custom was to put all the livers together in a butter boat. . . . The mullet have now deserted Weymouth for the coast of Cornwall.

The Art of Dining, by A.H., 1853.

Mullet livers are the desirable bit, although the whole fish is good. They are still available, but mostly imported. Red mullet should be cooked with the liver left inside, baked at gas mark 4–5 for 20–30 minutes with the herb or vegetable fennel, or simply with lemon and butter.

Baked Trout

Trout must have been fished from the streams and rivers of Dorset since the prehistoric period, but today those found in the shops will have come from one of the fifteen or so trout farms in the county. Fished or farmed, they are delicious cooked simply, which is probably why none of the Dorset cookery books give recipes.

Dan Stembridge is in the 1911 Bridport Directory as a fishmonger and fruiterer. This postcard of about 1910 shows the huge range of willow baskets then used for produce. (Bridport Museum)

Dunford Fish and Chip Shop, Victoria Road, Dorchester, probably at Carnival time, c. 1960.

Printed recipe books of the eighteenth century suggest frying them in butter, and serving with fried parsley, a sauce of anchovy and white wine, garnished with lemon.

Baking is the easiest and best manner of cooking trout. Wrap the gutted fish in foil, with a knob of butter and a couple of slices of lemon. Bake at gas mark 5–6 for 15 to 25 minutes (assuming the trout weighs about ½lb). Dill or fennel can be added, or flaked almonds, or sliced mushrooms.

Smoked Trout

The quickest way to cook this is to grill, needing only 3–6 minutes a side. Lemon juice and butter can be used on them. Poaching is also possible, using a mixture say of white wine and water. The fish need only simmer for 4–6 minutes.

Smoked trout is available locally, and is a delicious alternative to smoked mackerel.

Leading the bull at Lower Farm, Kington Magna, c. 1910. The farmer wears a dress-like smock, used for milking.

Meat

Dorset Horn sheep. From Moss Green Days *(1947).*

Meat

Many of the eighteenth-century (and earlier) recipes are designed to improve meat which was going off. One recipe is blatant: 'To make sausages from stinking meat.' Vinegar was commonly used to mask taints, and thankfully none of these recipes are needed today. Much of the meat would simply have been roasted on a spit in front of the fire, but there are more complex recipes for stuffed meat, stews and so on. Boiled meat (rather a misnomer as it is simmered) is uncommon today, but was universal. Good recipes for cuts now seen as less desirable, like breast of lamb, evolved because the whole carcass had to be used up. From Tyneham:

Roast Collared Breast of Mutton

TO COLLAR A BREAST OF MUTTON
Bone and skin your Mutton cut off the neck and and a little way done, and put where the long bones are wanting. Role it down with a Roling pin, to make the Meat lie smooth, then Wet the mutton all over with Yolks of Eggs, then strew seasoning all over which must be Thyme Marjoram Lemon peel and Samphire, all chopt small, grated Bread Pepper Salt and Nutmeg mixt altogether, Role it tie and bind it in a Cloath, boil it two hours and a half cut it in 4 or 5 pieces, put in your Dish, pour yr Sauce over it, a strong brown Gravy made as thick as thick cream.

Collaring means to tie in a roll, with stuffing, a very effective way of using a thin cut like breast. Ask the butcher for a good breast of lamb (or mutton if available), boned. They are very cheap. Another recipe in the same book includes bacon rolled with the meat.

one breast of lamb, boned	bread made into crumbs; or good
egg yolk	pinch thyme and marjoram, lemon
stuffing: good pinch nutmeg and	peel, breadcrumbs; or add chopped
allspice, thinly sliced lemon peel,	mushroom to the mixture
about ½lb bacon, one good slice	

Wet the lamb with the egg yolk, lay the stuffing ingredients on, and roll up. Tie up with string, and roast at gas mark 6 for an hour.

   If the joint is not tied up it tends to unroll in cooking. The composition of the stuffing is infinitely variable, but I think lemon peel goes better with spices than herbs. A very tasty roast, good cold as well. Boiling is also possible. Best to make a stock with the bones, then cook the meat in it. About an hour and a quarter's simmering cooks it.

Beef Olives

Beef olives, thin slices of meat and a spicy stuffing rolled up, are known from medieval times. There are several versions in the Tyneham cookery book, some for veal and others mutton:

VEAL OLIVES A PRITTY DISH
Cut thin slices of a Leg of Veal, hack them with a back of a Knife, lay forced meat over the slices Role them up and sew them and spit them the short way upon a Lark Spit, and Lard them with bacon Rub them over with the Yolk of an Egg and Sprinkle Crumbs of bread on them, with a little Lemon peel cut fine a little Nutmeg and salt, the sauce must be thick Gravy with Morels, Truffles Mushrooms and forced Meat balls.

For Two

3 or 4 slices of bacon
peel of one lemon
marjoram

about ½lb thin slices of beef
egg yolk

Put the bacon, lemon peel and marjoram on the meat, using the egg yolk to keep it there. Roll up. Roast with a little fat at gas mark 4 for about 30 minutes. Alternative fillings are beef suet, savory, nutmeg and a little bread, all mixed with egg yolk; forced meat made as the Tyneham recipe below but with only two or three of the herbs and spices; or bread, suet and grated lemon peel.

Lemon peel is surprisingly good with meat, especially in the bacon version.

Boiled Lamb with Caper Sauce

Apart from ham boiled meat is uncommon today. Eighteenth-century cookery books are full of it, and it remained popular into the twentieth century. Thomas Hardy's favourite dinner was boiled lamb with caper sauce, a classic.

leg of lamb

salt, pepper, allspice, water

Put the meat in a saucepan with just enough water to cover, with a little salt, pepper and allspice, whole or ground. (Other spices, e.g. cloves, can be used, but not too much of any if you are going to use the water as stock afterwards.) Bring slowly to the boil, remove the scum with a slotted spoon, and simmer for 20 minutes to the pound and 20 minutes over. Like ham, the lamb should just simmer, not boil wildly. If part

Feeding lambs at a Bridport farm, c. 1890. (Bridport Museum)

of the joint remains when it has been carved, return it to the cooking water to cool. This prevents shrinking, and is a good idea with ham too. When all is cold, it can be removed.

CAPER SAUCE (FOR ½ PINT)

1oz fat

1oz flour

¼ pint milk

¼ pint of the cooking water from the lamb

about 2 tablespoons pickled capers

Melt the fat, add the flour and mix together well. Gradually add the liquid until the consistency you require is reached, add the capers and cook for 5 minutes.

Capers have an unusual strong taste: they are most familiar in sauce tartare. The meat is good from boiled lamb: tasty, firm and not greasy, but the joint does not look pretty. The cooking water makes good stock for soups and stews. Leg is the best joint for boiling as it is less fatty than, for example, shoulder. Good with Dorset Norfolk Dumplings (see p. 93)

Boiled Chicken and Sauce

Elderly fowls used to be sold specifically for boiling, but are less common today. An ordinary chicken can be used, and like boiled lamb the meat is firm and tasty.

a chicken	a good pinch of ground
salt, pepper	mace and nutmeg (optional)
2 tablespoons lemon juice	

Put all the ingredients in a saucepan with enough water to cover the chicken. Bring slowly to the boil and simmer for 20 minutes to the pound; 35 minutes to the pound if it is an old bird. Vegetables can be cooked in with the chicken, adding them the correct amount of time before the end of cooking, e.g. 20 minutes before the end for carrots, 5 minutes for leeks.

From Tyneham a complex sauce:

SAUCE FOR BOYLD CHICKEN
Take a Liver Boyld and Mash it with Butter a Spoonful of White Wine another of Gravy some cream, if you like it a little Anchovy, some Lemon juce and Peel cut small be sure let it just boyl, a few Oysters are a good addition, the Wine and Lemon juice put in just before you send it up.

Rather too many flavourings: oysters were so cheap that they were added to most sauces.

SAUCE FOR CHICKEN	
a chicken liver	tablespoon lemon juice
½ pint chicken stock, or half stock half	zest of half a small lemon
white wine	

Boil the chicken liver in the stock with all the other ingredients. When the liver is cooked, liquidise and bring to the boil.

This has a good sharp flavour: an anchovy strip would make it saltier. It could be thickened. Lemon and liver are good together, and half a pound of chicken livers, fried and then baked in the oven in a sauce of ¼ pint chicken stock, zest of a lemon and 2 tablespoons of lemon juice for 10 to 20 minutes at gas mark 3 works well. Probably best thickened. With rather more stock and liquidised after cooking, it would make a very rich soup.

Jugged Hare or Steak

Jugged hare is the one survivor of the easiest way to stew meat without an oven. Really the technique is that of boiled puddings, with the meat and flavourings sealed in a container heated by boiling water. From Mrs Chafin's late seventeenth-century recipe book:

TO BOIL A HARE IN A GUGG
Cutt her in small pieces and season her with a penny worth of Cloves and mace together with a little nutmeg and peper and salt, rub every piece as you put it into the Gugg; put about the middle of the Gugg a bunch of Sweet hirbes and a onion sliced, and one Anchovey, with a pint of White Wine, or Cyder, put the Gugg into a kettle of Watter and boyl it 3 hours, lett not the Watter be above the Gugg, and as the Watter boils away keep it filld with hott watter, when it have boil'd its time, take it up, and poure it upon the Hare, and squeeze a Lemon over it, the Gugg must be keep Close Stop'd.

At Tyneham the hare was jugged with nutmeg in cider or claret, and at Bloxworth port wine and walnut catchup was used with mace, cloves and anchovies.

hare, jointed, or 1½lb braising steak, cut into large pieces	1½oz fat and flour
½ teaspoon ground cloves and nutmeg	about ½ pint of wine or cider for steak, 1 pint for hare
a little flour	4–8 strips of anchovy, and a teaspoon mixed herbs (optional)
a large onion (about ½lb), sliced	

Season the meat with the spices mixed with a little flour, fry to brown it with the sliced onions. Put the meat and onion in a jug (probably a lidded pot is best, or even a lidded bowl as used for steamed puddings). Add the flour to the fat in the frying pan, make a roux, and steadily add the wine or cider so that it thickens, and pour the sauce over, add the anchovies, chopped up. Put the jug, with its lid on, in a saucepan of water, so that the water comes two-thirds of the way up the jug. Bring to the boil, and keep boiling for 3 hours (2–2½ for steak), topping the water up several times with boiling water.

This could be cooked in a casserole in the oven at gas mark 1–2 for 2–2½ hours, as indeed the Bloxworth recipe specifies.

Very tasty made with braising steak, spicy and rich. The anchovies do enhance it, and it is good made with anchovies and stock in place of the cider or wine.

A butcher in the market house at Dorchester in the 1920s. Below the town hall was the traditional spot for butchers in many towns – at Dorchester they were moved into a new market house in 1865 just behind the town hall.

Stuffing

'A pudding for hare' from Tyneham makes a good stuffing.

A Bit of Apple and Lemon peel Nutmeg and Salt dryed Crums of bread a small bit of Onion a leaf or two or sweet Marjoram mix'd with a good piece of butter, only plain Melt'd butter in yr Dish.

2oz onions	pinch of nutmeg and salt
a little butter	4oz breadcrumbs
4oz cooking apple	½ teaspoon marjoram
zest or chopped peel from half a lemon	an egg (optional)

67

Chop the onion finely and fry it in the butter. Peel, core and chop the cooking apple finely; mix all ingredients together. If wanted for balls of stuffing, or if it won't stick together, add a beaten egg. The original recipe called for dried breadcrumbs, but fresh are fine.

Good for stuffing chicken, or baked on its own in a dish for about ½–¾ hr at gas mark 4.

Meat Pies

Meat pies were one of the specialities of the country when I was a boy. I don't mean the unimaginative things like pork pies and veal and ham pies. They can be made in factories, and even in wartime they were the most popular eating material in railway station buffets. I mean real food like pigeon pie or rook pie. They cannot be made now because the pigeon or the rook are only relatively minor ingredients, there must be some fat bacon, mushrooms and hard boiled eggs. The trouble is that they were not being made before the war when the ingredients were readily available. It was too much trouble to skin a rook and cut up the best bits and make the pastry, when a factory made pork pie could be purchased at any store. Perhaps the best pie of the lot was made from lambs tails. Lamb tail pie also contains fat bacon and eggs. Eaten hot the gravy is better than anything I have ever tasted, while if the pie is allowed to cool the gravy sets into a delicious jelly.

Ralph Wightman, 1947

Rooks and pigeons are difficult to obtain, and I'm not sure the fatty bacon (needed because the rook and pigeon are dry meat) would be popular today.

Pasties or pastries, the meat pies of earlier times, could be massive. One recipe from the Bragges of Sadborow for making beef pie attempts to imitate venison, and expects 10lb of meat in one piece. The meat was marinated in sugar and then claret, wrapped in pastry with butter on top of the meat. Especially large peels (wooden paddles) were made to lift these great pies in and out of the oven.

As with suet puddings, it is better to partially cook the meat for a pie, so that the pastry does not have to suffer a couple of hours in the oven. Really there are two types of pie: those with pastry above and below, and those with pastry only above. Those with double pastry are good hot or cold.

The Filling

about 1½lb braising steak, or diced pork (shoulder is good)	1–2oz fat
	⅓–½ pint stock
1oz flour	¼lb mushrooms or ½lb tomatoes (optional)

Roll the meat in flour, and fry in the fat to brown all over. Add the flour, mix with the fat, and slowly add the stock to make a thick sauce. Put meat and sauce in a saucepan and cook in the oven at gas mark 1 for about an hour until the meat is nearly done.

The Pastry

2½oz lard	5oz wholemeal flour
2½oz butter	teaspoon baking powder
5oz plain white flour	cold water to mix

Rub the fats and flours and baking powder together thoroughly. Mix with cold water to make a stiff dough (less than ⅛ pint). Form into a ball and leave in the fridge for half an hour. Butter and flour a 10-inch plate with a deepish middle. Line with half the pastry, put meat in with tomatoes or mushrooms if used. Put in as much of the sauce as nearly fills the base and cover with the rest of the pastry. The top can be

Higgins butcher's shop, Dorchester, c. 1910. He sold frozen New Zealand lamb, cheese (to the right of the door) and some groceries. This is a Christmas photograph – there is mistletoe above the door.

brushed with egg yolk or milk, and ground black pepper sprinkled on. Bake at gas mark 6 for about 45 minutes.

If some of the sauce was left over when filling, reheat as gravy to serve with the pie.

Meat pies are better with a robust pastry like this one. Good hot with succulent vegetables like leeks or cauliflower, or cold with a salad.

Rabbit Pie

about 3lb rabbit joints	prunes (soaked), 6oz mushrooms;
½lb streaky bacon, or belly of pork	lemon peel; sage; a pinch of mace
seasoned flour	and nutmeg (optional)
1oz flour, 1½oz fat	For lid: pastry made from about
about ½ pint good stock	4oz flour
a couple of onions; ½lb	

Roll the joints of rabbit in seasoned flour, and fry to brown as much of the surfaces as possible. Remove from the frying pan and mix the ounce of flour with the fat to make a roux. Add the stock steadily, stirring till it thickens. Put the rabbit and stock

Rural butchers also put on a fine display. Here is Abbotsbury in the late nineteenth century.

in an ovenproof saucepan (with thinly pared lemon peel spice or herbs if used) and cook in the oven at gas mark 1–2 for about 2 hours until the meat is virtually cooked. Add the prunes, mushrooms or onions, if used, put all in a dish, add the pastry lid and bake at gas mark 6 for about 30 minutes, reducing the temperature after the pastry is done to gas mark 3 to continue cooking the rabbit if necessary.

Large quantities of rabbit are needed because it is very bony, and the fat pork or bacon helps to stop the meat being too dry. Some flavouring is a good idea: onions and sage, or prunes and lemon are effective combinations. Pastry made with 6oz of dripping to 1lb of flour is suitable for meat pies, but any other version can be used. To get round the boniness, a pasty-like pie can be made, which is also good cold.

Rabbit Pasty

Cook the rabbit as above, but after cooking in the oven allow to cool and remove the meat from the bones. Mix this with about one-third its weight chopped streaky bacon, and add mushrooms or onions, chopped up. Use this mixture as the filling for a top-and-bottom pie, along with as much of the gravy the rabbit was cooked in as you can get in. Cook at gas mark 6 for about 30 minutes, until the pastry is done.

Casseroled rabbit is really just the same as the pie, but without a pastry lid. Allow 2½–3 hours cooking in the oven.

Mutton Casserole

Veal, mutton and beef are found in casserole recipes in the eighteenth-century cookery books, often with flavourings not commonly found today. Lemon, orange and anchovy are used, along with a variety of spices. From Tyneham:

A HARRICO OF MUTTON

Take a Neck of Mutton cut it in stakes put it in a Stewpan with slices of Carrott, Turnep and onions, sweet Herbs and whole peper, let it stew over a slow Fire till the Mutton is of a Brown colour then add some good broth or Gravy and Stew the Stakes till they are very tender. Take 3 carrots 5 Turneps cut them in dices and boyl them in fair water till they are Tender, take small Onions no.24 and boyl likewise, when done take the Turneps Carrots and Onions put them in a Stew pan with 3 Anchovies some shred Lemon Peel and just simmer over the fire till the Anchovies are dissolved, then thicken it up with butter done with flower, you may Squeeze in half a lemon, place the stakes round the dish and pour the Ragoo over them, garnish with Horse Radish and Lemon.

Mutton is virtually unobtainable today, but stewing lamb makes a good substitute. Eighteenth-century casseroles seem always to have the vegetables cooked separately, which is unnecessary.

2–2½lb stewing lamb	½lb turnips
seasoned flour	½lb carrots
1–2oz fat	4 strips anchovy
¾lb shallots (or onions)	large lemon
1½oz flour	teaspoon mixed herbs and
¾–1 pint stock	teaspoon horseradish (optional)

Roll the meat in seasoned flour and fry both sides till brown. Put the meat in a casserole. Fry the peeled shallots or peeled and sliced onions, then add the flour to the fat, make a roux, and slowly add the stock to thicken. Put the shallots and thickened stock into the casserole along with the peeled and chopped-up turnips and carrots, chopped-up anchovies, peel and juice of the lemon (and herbs and horseradish if used). Bring to the boil, put the oven at gas mark 1–2 for 2½–3 hours.

I prefer this with lemon and anchovy, without the herbs and horseradish, but this is a matter of taste. It is good either way.

Stewed Beef

TO STEW COLLOPS OF BEEF

Take the Buttock of Beef thin slices across the grain of the meat. Hack ym and fry them in sweet Butter, and being fryed fine and brown, put them in a Pipkin with some strong Broath a little Clarret Wine and some Nutmeg, stew it very tender, and half an hour before you Dish it put to it some good Gravy Elder Vinegar and a Clove or two, when you serve it put some juce of Oranges, and 3 or 4 slices on it, stew the Gravy somewhat thick, and put into it, when you dish it some beaten flower.

A rich simple casserole from Tyneham. I am not clear whether elder vinegar is vinegar flavoured with elderflowers, or vinegar made from elderberry wine, or flavoured with elderberries. I think any of them would do.

1½lb stewing beef	half a nutmeg, grated
seasoned flour	pinch ground cloves
1½oz fat	A dash of vinegar
1oz flour	Half an orange
About ¾ pint good stock, or half stock, half claret	a little elderberry wine, or juice from elderberries (optional)
5 or 6 tablespoons orange juice	

Driving animals to market led to many problems – in 1953 three heifers decided to visit Dyer's Grocery in Dorchester, and had to be driven out through the front door.

Sheep and cattle penned in the main street at Bridport in 1913. All towns held markets like this, but Bridport had a late revival of selling animals in the main road when their market site was built over in 1913. They soon had another one. (Bridport Museum)

Roll the meat in seasoned flour, and fry both sides until brown. Add the flour to the fat, make a roux, and steadily add the stock to thicken it. Put all ingredients except the half orange in a casserole, and cook at gas mark 1–2 for 2½–3 hours. Before serving slice the half orange on top.

The original is for slices of meat, but chopped pieces are fine. Very spicy, and would be good with baked potatoes and a green vegetable.

Watercress and Beef Casserole

1–2 bunches watercress	seasoned flour
1–1¼ pints stock	1½oz fat
1½lb lean stewing beef, in cubes	1½oz flour
About 6–8oz onions, chopped	

Wash the watercress. Put in liquidiser with ½ pint of stock, and liquidise. (If you do not have a liquidiser, chop the watercress). Roll the meat in seasoned flour, fry in the fat with the onions till brown. Add the flour to make a roux, then steadily add the stock stirring all the while. Add the watercress, put into a casserole and cook in the oven at gas mark 1 for 2½–3 hours. Baked potatoes cook very well at the same time. This is a good casserole, the watercress flavouring the meat.

A market held in the streets of Bridport, January 1913. (Bridport Museum)

74

Boiled Puddings

Traditionally suet puddings and some batters were boiled in a well-floured pudding cloth wrapped around the mixture, leaving enough room for it to swell. This was ideal for open-fire cooking, as it could be added to a cauldron of boiling water in which everything else was cooked. Vegetables could be kept separate in nets, and meat boiled at the same time as a sweet, savoury or even neutral pudding was cooked. The cloth would have to be well cleaned and scalded before re-use. It is not a convenient method today since we are not used to cauldron cooking.

During the nineteenth century pudding basins were used, covered by a cloth which was tied under the rim with string and knotted over the top. The string or the knotted cloth made a handle to lift the pudding from its saucepan of boiling water. An ordinary lidded saucepan was used, with a wire tray inside to keep the pudding basin off the bottom of the saucepan. Again the cloth needs scalding after use.

Today there are inexpensive plastic bowls made especially for steaming, in several sizes and with close-fitting lids. They are ideal for their purpose, and while they do not have the old-fashioned appeal of cloths and ceramic basins, they make life a lot easier, and are an encouragement to make steamed puddings. The method is the same using either a ceramic or plastic basin – when lidded, the basin is placed in a saucepan containing enough water to come about halfway up its side, standing on a wire tray. The water is brought to the boil, and kept just boiling. It will need topping up with boiling water two or three times during the time needed to cook the pudding.

Steak and Kidney Pudding and Boiled Chicken Pudding

Pastry for Large Pie

12oz self-raising flour	pinch salt
6oz suet	scant ½ pint cold water

Mix all the ingredients together with enough cold water to make a stiffish paste. Butter and flour a large (about 3-pint) pudding basin and line with the pastry, keeping some to make a lid (it swells up so allow it room).

FILLING

The classic is steak and kidney, about 1½lb stewing steak with about 3–4oz chopped kidney. Steak and tomato, chicken and celery or chicken and mushroom are also good.

To avoid the 3 or 4 hours boiling needed if raw meat is used, pre-cook the meat or chicken. Roll the meat in flour with a little salt and pepper and fry until browned.

Add 1½oz flour, making a roux with the frying fat, and then add about ⅓ pint of stock slowly so that it thickens with the roux. Cook gently in a saucepan for 15–20 minutes, or place in the oven at gas mark 1 for ¾–1 hour to partially cook the meat. (This can be done the day before.) Put into the lined bowl; mushrooms, celery or tomatoes should be added at this stage. Cover with the lid, and boil for 2 hours. If the meat is large, e.g. chicken breasts, add ½ hour to cooking time.

Pheasant with Game Sauce

Game birds are hardly mentioned in the manuscript cookery books of the county, presumably because they were simply roasted. Tyneham does have:

SAUCE FOR PARTRIDGE OF PHEASANT
Take clear good gravy and boil two or three shallots in it, then put a little vinegar and Chion Pepper and bring it up in a Sauce Boat.

Game Sauce

½ pint good strong stock   dash of vinegar, pinch of cayenne

2 or 3 shallots

Cook the shallots in the stock, add the vinegar and cayenne pepper and serve. Good, strong-tasting shallots make this spicy sauce distinctive, but at a pinch onion could be used.

Pheasants and partridges, if young and tender, are best simply roasted at gas mark 7 for 20 minutes to the pound, with 10 minutes over. A good knob of butter should be placed inside the bird, and streaky bacon put over the breast. The bacon should be removed for the last 10 minutes so the breast crisps.

Pheasant Casserole

Take any sort of fowls or birds fill them with forc'd meat, Lard them and half Roast ym have ready a good quantity of Gravy and stew them in it till they are enough. Season the Gravy with a little pepper salt Mace Nutmeg Sweet Herbs Anchovys Shallots and Lemon Peel when then they Stew'd enough put in a bit of butter and serve it up. Garnish with forced Meat Lemon and barberrys.

A good method of cooking older birds, but like many of the eighteenth-century recipes, this one from Tyneham has so many flavours that they overpower one another. Half roasting seems rather elaborate for a casserole: frying is enough.

a pheasant	1oz flour
seasoned flour	about ½ pint stock
about 1½oz fat	

Roll the pheasant in seasoned flour and fry it, turning as much as possible so all the outside is browned. Remove from the pan, add the flour to the fat, make a roux and gradually add the stock, stirring. Put the pheasant in an ovenproof pan just large enough for it, add the thickened stock (should be enough to cover the bird) and cook at gas mark 1 for a couple of hours.

A pinch of mace and nutmeg added to the stock, with a few chopped shallots and either a couple of anchovies or lemon peel are good flavourings. Alternatively 'sweet herbs', parsley, thyme, marjoram and savory could be used, along with the shallots and anchovies. Barberries are used in several of the Tyneham recipes: they are the fruits of *Berberis vulgaris* and were probably cultivated rather than wild.

A modern recipe for pheasant replaces the stock by cider, and includes about a pound of cooking apples, peeled, cored and sliced. Chicken joints could be used instead of pheasant.

Forced Meat

The Tyneham recipe for forced meat is similar to that given below for sweetbreads, but with more herbs and spices:

Take a little Veal mince it very small with a pretty deal of Beef suet, beat it well in a Morter and as you beat it, break in two Eggs then mix in some sweet herbs chop'd small, such as Lemon Thyme a little Savory and sweet Majoram, mix all together and season it with salt, a little pepper Cloves Mace Nutmeg and Lemon peel, grate in a little bread, take some fine flower in your hand when you role them up, for frying.

I think this is better on its own, fried or roasted, than as a stuffing. If minced meat is used no extra fat is needed for these prototype burgers.

1lb minced meat	zest of one lemon
pinch salt, pepper, mace nutmeg	pinch cloves or pinch marjoram,
7 tablespoons breadcrumbs	savory and thyme (optional)
1 egg	

Mix the meat with the lemon zest, herbs or spice and bread, whisk the egg and add it. Either fry in thin cakes for about 5 minutes each side, or form into balls and bake in a metal dish with a little fat in the oven at gas mark 6 for about 20 minutes.

I find the cloves rather overpowering, and prefer them with either lemon and spice, or herbs. They can be eaten hot or cold.

Rissoles

A pound of veal, better than a quarter of a pound of beef suit, beat these in a stone mortar very fine together season them with pepper and salt, work the into the fashion of small sweetbreads, dip them into the yolks of two eggs, fry them in a good quantity of dry'd suit of a fine light brown colour as near as you can to them you broil melt better and garnish your dish or plates with orange or lemon.

An early eighteenth-century recipe from the Bragges of Sadborow. Sweetbreads really means a particular type of offal. They may have been made from raw meat or from cooked. Rissoles are useful to use up the remains of roast lamb, or other meat, and they are surprisingly good with slices of lemon or orange.

8oz cooked meat, minced (if lean add 2oz suet) ½lb potatoes, cooked and mashed	1 egg pickle or chutney, a small onion, parsley (optional)

Mix the meat, mashed potato, and flavouring if used, together with the beaten egg. Form into flat cakes, and fry for about 5 minutes each side. Serve with slices of lemon or orange.

Tomatoes, mushrooms or more onion can be added, preferably well chopped or else the rissoles will tend to fall apart. A little lemon or orange zest in them is unusual, but good. The quantities and even proportions are pretty arbitrary.

Vegetables are barely mentioned in the early cookery books, but somehow one imagines that they were overcooked. The *Housekeeper's Receipt Book* (1813) is a shock. The book sensibly recommends careful cleaning and then cooking quickly in boiling water: 'All kinds of vegetables should have a little crispness, and therefore must not be boiled too much.'

Bacon and Ham

A pig was the cottage animal, easy to keep on a small amount of ground, and happy to eat nearly anything. Bacon was virtually the only meat the labourers of Dorset ate in the nineteenth century, and traditionally flitches of bacon hanging in the

CECIL COX'S
FAMILY BUTCHER,
AND
Provision Merchant,
HIGH STREET, EAST,
DORCHESTER.

PICKLED TONGUES.   CORNED BEEF.

Manufacturer of the Celebrated Cambridge Sausages.

FINE MILD BREAKFAST BACON,

HAMS OF THE CHOICEST CURE.

FIRST CLASS CHEDDAR AND
OTHER CHEESE.

Butcher's advertisement of 1875.

fireplace were admired as far better than any picture on the wall. Pork is easily preserved by salting and smoking, turning it into durable bacon or ham which could be used over a long period. Traditionally everything from the pig is useful, except the squeak. In 1947 Ralph Whitman was nostalgic about pre-war bacon:

> The day the pig was killed was a great occasion. The slaughtering, scalding and scraping was done by the village butcher who paid a solemn professional visit to the farm for the job. I have often thought since that it would have been much simpler to take the pig to the butcher's premises where certain facilities existed, and then to bring the meat home for curing. It may be that the butcher preferred the outing, plus the abundance of good food and drink, he got at the farm. It may be that he enjoyed the admiration evoked by his skilful surgery. Or, of course, it may be that we were just making sure that we got our pig and our whole pig, with no alien bits from his abattoir. Whatever the cause, that is the way it was always done, and it involved a terrific upheaval in the home. Great coppers of boiling water were necessary. The long table in the larder had to be cleared and scrubbed. Bowls of all sorts and sizes had to be found and scoured in readiness for all sorts of dark and terrible uses. Nothing of a pig was wasted by

the good farm housewife. As far as I can remember the actual curing was done by leaving the joints in a brine of salt and saltpetre with sundry other ingredients which were a close family secret. The hams were preserved by rubbing them daily with dry salt and leaving them covered with dry salt. Later on the hams and the sides of bacon were hung up in the big kitchen chimney and smoked. Thirty years ago there was scarcely a farmhouse in the West of England without half a pig up the chimney.

According to the seventeenth- and eighteenth-century Dorset recipe books salt and saltpetre were used to make bacon, sometimes with sugar. The back of the big was used for bacon, the legs for hams, which were treated the same way. Either the pork was left in a brine (sometimes made from beer rather than water) for a couple of weeks, or it was rubbed with salt daily. Afterwards it was smoked in the chimney, woodsmoke being recommended. A late seventeenth-century recipe from Parnham suggests 'a poor persons Chimney is best because their fires are not too great a heat'.

The cottager's pigs were fed on small potatoes, vegetable peelings, apples and any kitchen scraps, but in order to fatten them barley meal was needed. Often millers would allow the meal on credit, calling in the loan in pork when the pig was killed. This led to the strange statement 'We're killing half a pig tomorrow', meaning not partial slaughter, but partial ownership. Commercially pigs were often kept by dairy farms, as they could be fed on the skimmed milk left from butter production, or the whey from cheesemaking.

Most of the bacon was simply sliced and fried, but sometimes boiled. In Hardy's short story 'Old Mrs Chundle' she feeds the curate on her own dinner 'taters and cabbage, boiled with a scantling of bacon'. The curate admired the dinner: 'the vegetables had just been brought in from the garden and had been well cooked over a wood fire – the only way to cook a vegetable – and the bacon was well boiled'. Hardy's nostalgia for open fire cooking comes over here.

Some recipes were designed to make the bacon go further. Kathleen Winter Saunders, writing of the later 1920s on Portland, described how

instead of meat we had pea soups made from bacon bones and a really tasty filling dish was a streaky bacon, onion and potato pie. First you had a layer of onions sliced at the bottom of the dish, on top of that a layer of sliced thin potato rings, topped up with a row of streaky bacon, this was repeated until the dish was as full as you needed, baked with a little water to start if off at the bottom of the dish. It was cooked in the oven of the kitchen range and dished up with wild spinach which Father collected by the sackful from the Railway or Weymouth Road. It really was a lively tasty dish and with a bit of suet duff we had a grand meal.

A Child of Chiswell Remembers

Portland Bacon

1lb onions	½lb back bacon
1lb potatoes	¼lb streaky bacon

Put layers of sliced onion, peeled and sliced potatoes and back bacon in a fireproof dish. Use the streaky bacon for the top layer. Put ¾–½ inch of water in the bottom of the dish, and place in a low oven (gas mark 1–2) for about two hours.

The streaky bacon drips fat through the rest, and gets rather crisp. Streaky or back could be used throughout. It is not fussy and can easily be cooked in the bottom of the oven while something else is being cooked at a higher temperature. Cheese could be grated over the top. This feeds four people.

Sausages with Apple

1lb sausages (strong-tasting ones)	1lb potatoes, peeled and sliced
½lb cooking apples, peeled, cored and chopped	dripping or other fat
½lb onions, peeled and sliced	

The quantities do not need to be exact. Put the sausages and chopped apple on the bottom of an ovenproof saucepan or dish. Cover with layers of sliced onion and potato. Put about 2 tablespoons of water in, and cook covered at gas mark 1–2 for 1½ hours. Uncover, dot with dripping or other fat and continue cooking uncovered for another hour.

This substantial dish is derived from the Portland bacon recipe, and is very easy, and very tasty. The apple and sausage combine well. It can be cooked in the bottom of the oven while things that need a higher temperature can cook above it. A few slices of streaky bacon may be put on top to add the necessary fat.

Thomas Hardy's Meat Loaf

There are many recipes for potted meat in the Dorset recipe books, mostly simple mixtures of minced meat cooked in butter. The sausage recipe from Max Gate is more like a meat loaf, and is a useful dish, good hot or cold. The bacon makes this recipe distinctive. The original was boiled in a cloth for three hours, and then coated with breadcrumbs. Baking with slices of bacon around it is more practical and gives a better result because excess fat can be removed.

¾lb streaky bacon
8oz bread (brown or granary is best)
1lb minced beef
½ teaspoon each ground mace,
   nutmeg and black pepper

2 eggs, beaten
4 good thick slices back bacon

Remove the rind from the streaky bacon, and mince. Mince the bread. Mix the minced beef, bread, minced bacon and spices together and then mix in the eggs. Line a loaf tin with the back bacon, cutting the slices to fit as necessary. Fill with the meat mixture. Bake at gas mark 3 for 1¼ hours. Excess fat will cook out of the meat and can be poured away after the cooking. To serve, turn out of the tin, so that it appears covered in bacon.

Good hot, perhaps with a tomato sauce, and equally good cold with a salad. The recipe is easily varied, using different meats, other spices, or even grated lemon rind. It is very filling, and the amounts above are ample for eight people.

Venison

Venison has been a special meat, used for feasts and celebrations, from at least medieval times. It is often marinated, but if the joint is from a youngish animal simple roasting is fine. Deer are once again common in Dorset, and venison can be bought quite easily.

The meat is strongly flavoured, and delicious. It should be roasted for 25 minutes to the pound at gas mark 5 and the traditional marinade consists of

½ bottle red wine
¼ pint olive oil
⅛ pint wine vinegar

2 tablespoons crushed peppercorns
one onion, diced
a few bay leaves

The joint is submerged in this marinade overnight, and then removed and roasted. Beer can be substituted for the wine, and for large joints all the quantities need to be increased. The joint, marinated or not, can be surrounded with peeled, cored and sliced cooking apples, and then roasted. Traditionally redcurrant jelly is served with venison.

Sadborow has 'Venison Mutton' using a boned loin of mutton marinaded in 'a tumbler of port wine' with ½oz mace, a little pepper and salt. After a day it was stewed in the liquor for an hour which was served as the sauce.

Pudding

Feeding the chickens in a Dorset farmyard about 1890. Eggs were the vital ingredient for many puddings.

Puddings

There are a surprising number of unfamiliar good puddings in the eighteenth-century cookery books, especially those from Bloxworth and Tyneham. Custards, bread puddings, cheesecakes, syllabubs and so on use local produce mixed with expensive imports like almonds, currants and other dried fruits. Spices were freely used, especially cloves, mace and nutmeg. Almost all are too sweet for modern tastes, so some of the sugar has been omitted.

Pastry

> 8oz butter (or 6oz margarine: just under ¼ pint cold water
> add 1 teaspoon baking powder to flour)
> 1lb plain white flour
> or 12oz plain white flour and 4oz
> wholemeal flour (see note on flour)

Cut the butter into smallish pieces and mix with the flour. Either rub in by hand or by machine, but it must be mixed very thoroughly. Add enough cold water to make a stiff paste and leave it for ½ an hour in the fridge. Roll out to a thin sheet on a floured surface. Bake at gas mark 6.

A fine eighteenth-century pastry, good for all the sweet tarts given here. To bake blind, line the tin with pastry, put a sheet of baking foil inside, then beans to support the foil. Bake. Pastry made from 1lb flour will, used thinly, line 24 little tarts and 3–4 large ones (all without lids). Leaving the pastry in the fridge before using it does improve it. The margarine version has the same excellent texture, but does not taste as good.

SHORT CRUST (from Sadborow, early nineteenth century)
Mix one ¼oz of lump sugar pounded and sifted with 2oz of flour then rub in 1½oz of butter mix it up with as little water as possible so as to have it a stiff paste. Beat it a good deal with a rolling pin then roll it out and put it on the tart. It must be baked in a moderate oven.

I like the idea of pastry being beaten a good deal with a rolling pin, but apart from that this is a much more modern type of sweet pastry with a high fat content.

> 3oz butter   ½oz caster sugar
> 4oz flour   scant 2 tablespoons cold water

Use the butter straight from the fridge, and the better the butter, the better the pastry. Rub the butter into the flour – probably easier in a machine with such a high proportion of fat. Mix the sugar in, and add the water. Be careful not to overdo the rubbing-in if using a machine. Rest in the fridge for an hour. Roll out thinly and use for the top of a fruit pie, or for 16 little tarts. Very good filled with a delicate jelly like redcurrant. Bake at gas mark 6½ for 10–15 minutes for the little tarts, longer for big ones. Good just cooked, or slightly browned.

Also good with the sugar omitted for other pies. The pastry is definitely a Sunday-best version, crisp but somehow soft as well. A little lemon juice added to the water perhaps helps the savoury version. Good for cheesecakes, and wonderful with home-made jam or jelly.

Mr Clark's Sweet Pastry

Pastry made with eggs was considered old-fashioned by the early eighteenth century but it occurs in the Tyneham cookery book, and in a loose sheet in Mrs Machen's:

Mr Clarks past for sweet meat Tarts, Crocants etc. Take one pound of flower two ounces of sugar sifted two eggs three ounces of Butter mix yr butter flower and sugar well together then make a hole in the middle breake the eggs into it then mix the eggs and a little water together work with yr hand then mix it up pretty stiff with some more water after yr past is mixed let it lie a little role it out into sheets to sheet your patty pans and prick them with a fork or into wch shapes or other uses you are pleased to put them into if for tarts to Ice the lids brush them wel with a Brush diped in melted butter and dust them wel with some fine and sifted sugar Bake them in a middling oven after baked fill them with what sweetmeats you please.

Crocants was the word used in England to mean sweet French pastry.

½lb plain white flour	scant 1oz caster sugar
or 6oz plain white flour and 2oz	1 egg
wholemeal	About 1½ tablespoons cold water
1½oz butter	

Rub the flour and butter together thoroughly and add the sugar. Mix together with the egg and enough water to make a stiff paste. Leave it in the fridge for half an hour. Bake it at gas mark 5. Nice on top of fruit, or for little tarts with not-too-sweet filling, e.g. apple.

Flour

Until almost the present day white flour has been the ambition of all cooks, but up to the middle of the nineteenth century (when roller milling was introduced) it was virtually impossible to obtain. For authenticity in all the recipes plain white flour could be mixed with about a quarter wholemeal or brown flour or '81%' flour used (see Bread). In fact the recipes are fine made with plain white flour, or with all brown flour. Authenticity is a difficult subject: many of the recipes instruct one to dry the flour in front of the fire before using it, suggesting that it was always damp. Full authenticity would mean getting the flour damp, and then drying it out.

Almond Cheesecakes

Almonds have been popular in English cooking since the medieval period. They were always expensive, as they had to be imported. In many of the recipes their taste and texture is submerged, but these cheesecakes preserve both. They seem to be a local speciality as they are not found in the printed cookery books of the eighteenth century. The orange cheesecake recipe occurs at Tyneham and at Bloxworth, with only minor variations.

ORANGE CHEESE CAKES
Half a pd of sweet almonds blanched and beat very fine with Orange flower water half a pd of sugar sift'd, strew it by degrees, into the Almonds, three quartrs of a pd

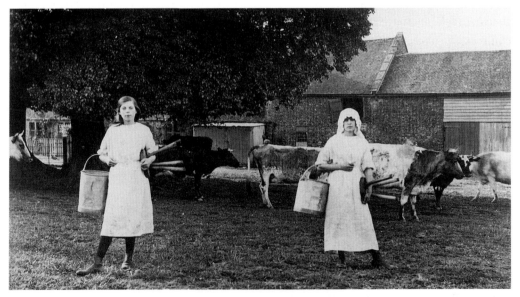

Milkers at Holwell in 1919 looking like Tess of the D'Urbervilles.

of melt'd butter let it stand till tis almost cold and then mix it with the Rine and Almonds the Rine must be of a large Sevel Orange pared pretty thick and boil'd tender Shifting the water till the bitterness is out, then beat it with the Almonds in a stone mortar to mix ym, 8 Yolks of Eggs and 4 Whites beat well, when you have put them in add the juice of yr Orange make the past light and very thin and fill ym full. Lemon will do as well as Orange.

Mrs Arnold's otherwise identical recipe in the Bloxworth cookery book replaces the orange peel with candied orange peel, and alternative recipes have rose water, but no orange or lemon peel.

A Sadborow version finishes 'any little thin bits of sweet meat, may be laid at the top' and she is right – the candied peel can be put in whole, or chopped on top.

Almond and Orange Cheesecake

½lb almonds (whole if you have a liquidiser, chopped otherwise)	½lb butter
rind 2 oranges or lemons (or 2 good tablespoonfuls well chopped marmalade) or 2oz candied citron	½oz sugar – a little more for lemons – less for marmalades
3 eggs	pastry made from ½lb flour
(enough for 3 8-inch tins)	tablespoon orange flower water (optional)

If you have a liquidiser, blanch the almonds (easiest way is to pour boiling water over them, leave for about 5 minutes, drain and pour more boiling water over. The skins then come off very easily). Put blanched almonds, thinly pared orange peel and eggs in the liquidiser with the orange flower water if used. Grind until the nuts are roughly chopped. (If not using a liquidiser beat the eggs, add chopped almonds and grated zest of the two oranges.) Melt the butter, allow to cool and mix all together. Put mixture in uncooked pastry cases: it is fine either thick or thin. Allow room for the mixture to rise. One of the Bloxworth recipes suggests 'lay some cross pieces of past in bars over it'. Bake at gas mark 6 for about 10 minutes, drop to gas mark 4 until cooked, about 35 minutes for large pies, 25 for small. It looks better if the top browns, but doesn't affect the taste.

Best made from whole almonds, an unusual, very successful recipe, good hot or cold, in large pans or small. Enough for 3 8-inch tins. A good alternative to mince pies.

Apricot and Almond Cheesecake

Apricot and almond cheesecake is good as well. Bottled apricots or dried ones soaked out are all right, but fresh are best.

6oz almonds	2 eggs
6oz apricots	6oz butter
	2oz sugar

Method as Almond and Orange. Check the sugar; you may need more or less depending on the tartness of the apricots. Makes 3 8-inch pies.

Orange and Apple Cheesecake

All the eighteenth-century apple pudding recipes add extra flavours to the apple. Orange water, orange zest or marmalade are very effective: surprisingly the orange does not overwhelm the apple. Quince is also used, and spices.

TO MAKE ORANGE CHEESECAKES (Bloxworth, Mid–later Eighteenth Century)
Take six or 7 large Apples and roast them thoroughly, and take all the pulp from them, or else coddle 4 or 5 and pulp them through a sieve. NB the roasted are the best. Take the yolks of six eggs well beaten; put to it a qr of a pd of white sugar, and to this quantity put a large tea-cup full of Orange Marmalade, beat it all well together; put a good crust in the pan and bake it a little before the Cheesecakes are put into them.

1½lb cooking apples	2 egg yolks, beaten
3oz dark marmalade	1½oz sugar

Bake the apples in the oven and then remove the pulp (this really is much better than stewing them). Chop the marmalade into small pieces. Mix with the beaten egg yolks and sugar. It is best to pre-cook the pastry shell, then add the filling and cook for about 20 minutes at gas mark 4. Very good rich apple and orange flavour.

Blandford Apple or Gooseberry Pudding

When the number of eggs and amount of sugar are adjusted (and the amount of butter inferred) this is a similar recipe, but with a slightly different flavour.

AN APPLE PUDDING TO BAKE FROM BLANDFORD, C. 1810
Take five Eggs have out one white beat them well with ounces of clarified butter a little Lemon or Orange peel grated, a bit of Nutmeg add to them the pulp of eight middling sized Apples beat all well together, with sugar to your taste beat with a silver spoon and bake it in puff paste – Gooseberries instead of Apples make a very good Pudding.

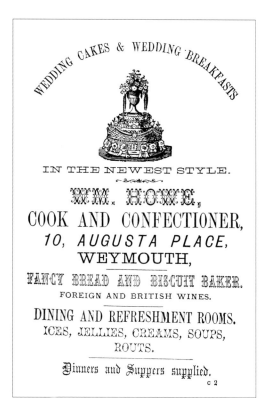

An 1875 advertisement from a high-class confectioner and cook. Buying in ready-made food is not new.

1lb cooking apples or gooseberries	lemon or orange zest
2 eggs	tiny pinch of nutmeg
2oz butter	2oz sugar

Method as Orange and Apple Cheesecake.

Apple Bread Pudding

Take of good Pippins number 12
If winter take 2 more
Then in a Skillet boil them well
And so take out the Core

Then take 2 manchett grated fine
12 yolks of eggs you use
Six of their Whites you must reserve
The other six refuse

Nearly half a well chosen nutmeg take
Not long from India brought
A little salt (the best I think
At Lymington is Wrought)

A Pound of butter next you take
Yellow as was the Ore
Which poets heretofore report
Was found on Tagus Shore

This in a silver saucepan you
Must melt oer gentle fire
And all in marble mortar mix
As artists do require.

With Lisbon sugar sweeten well
And to your pallat make it
Put all into a proper dish
And in the Oven bake it

Quite apart from poetic problems, this recipe from Bloxworth is difficult to decipher. Manchett should mean fine white bread, enriched with milk and eggs, not a quantity. The penny loaf or manchet probably weighed about 8oz, so perhaps 1lb bread is being added.

3 cooking apples (about 1¼lb)	4oz bread (about 4 slices from a large loaf)
3 eggs	4oz butter
pinch of salt	2oz sugar
pinch nutmeg (too much overwhelms the apple)	

Peel, core and cook the apples. Whisk the eggs, salt, nutmeg and sugar, add breadcrumbs (if using a mixer add the slices in whole, the mixer will crumb them). Melt the butter, allow to cool, add to mixture with the apple. Mix together, and bake in a well-buttered dish at gas mark 6 for about 45 minutes. Alternatively leave the slices of bread whole, use two to line the base of the dish, put the apples on top, then the other two slices of bread. Pour the egg, butter, sugar and spice mixture over the top. It will soak into the bread. The apple remains separate, encased in the bread. If the apple was chopped finely it could be used without being pre-cooked.

The result either way is a good pudding, very useful as a change when apples are abundant, and very different from other bread puddings.

Mother Eve's Pudding

> Would you have a good pudding pray mind what you are taught
> Take two penneth of eggs when they are twelve for a Groat
> Take of ye same fruit that Eve once did cozen
> Well pared and well Chop'd at least half a dozen
> Six Oz of Bread, let Moll eat ye Crust
> The Crumb must be grated as small as ye Dust
> Six Ounces of Currents from stem and stone sort
> Lest they stick in yr teeth and spoil all ye sport
> Six Ounces of Sugar wont make it too sweet
> Some salt and some Nutmeg ye whole will compleat
> Six hours let it boil without any flutter
> Nor is it quite finished without wine and sugar.

This Tyneham recipe perhaps pre-dates most of the recipes there as the groat, or 4d piece, ceased being issued in 1662 (or perhaps the author was desperate for a rhyme). The recipe produces a pudding similar to the other poem, but with the happy addition of currants. The proportions are about 2lb cooking apples, 6oz bread, 6oz currants, 6oz sugar, pinch of nutmeg and salt, and 5 eggs. Method as Apple Bread Pudding. The larger quantity of apples in this recipe makes it less like a bread pudding.

A slightly different version from Devonshire Buildings, Weymouth omits the currants and boils for a more reasonable 3 hours.

Friar's Omelet

A manuscript cookery book of 1854 from Bloxworth has an unusual omelette, which despite the name makes a delicious pudding.

Stew well some apples and well beat them up when cold put some lemon juice to it two eggs and a good tablespoonful of sugar, beat it all up together then pour into a dish which is well buttered.

½lb peeled and cored cooking apples	2 eggs
1oz caster sugar	lemon juice

Cook the chopped apples in as little water as possible. Allow to cool; drain and mash. Beat all ingredients together well. Cook for 15–20 minutes at gas mark 5 in a well-buttered metal dish.

Apple and egg are a good combination, and this makes a surprisingly filling dish. A handful of currants can be added, but if so halve the sugar. A Sadborow version adds 'as much brandy as suits the taste of ladies' and bakes it in pastry.

Egg and Apple Tarts

The Blandford book of about 1810 has a similar recipe:

TO MAKE AN APPLE PUDDING, MRS M. CASE
Take eight large Apples, put them in a pan of cold water, set them on the fire and let them scald till they are soft, pull off the skins and work them tho' a sieve and put in sugar to your taste, a quarter of a pound of Butter Oiled and worked well with the apples and sugar, six eggs well beaten and mixed with the apples, before it goes into the oven, a little rind of Limon grated and Puff Paste put in the dish.

1lb peeled and cored cooking apples	1–2oz caster sugar
2 eggs	lemon zest (optional)
2oz butter	

Cook the apples in as little water as possible and mash. Whisk the eggs, add the butter and apples and lemon zest. Sweeten to taste. Pour into large or small uncooked pastry cases and bake at gas mark 6 for 25–35 minutes. This will fill about three 8-inch cases, or 24 small ones.

Good with or without lemon, more interesting than simply apple on its own. The recipe could be adapted for other fruits if they were mashed or finely chopped.

Suet Puddings

Suet puddings, both sweet and savoury, are another survivor of early cooking. They are little made today, surprisingly as they are easy to produce, delicious and easy to vary. The cooking times are not exact: 1½ hours will cook a small one made with ½lb flour, but it will not spoil if cooked for another half hour or more (see notes on boiled puddings on p. 75).

Suet is shredded animal fat, which must always have been available, whereas the supply of butter (anyway more expensive) would have varied depending on the season. All the early recipes instruct one to 'chop it fine' or 'shred it small'. Today it is sold already shredded, and as an alternative vegetable suet is available and makes good pastry or pudding. There are very few suet recipes in the surviving manuscript cookery books, presumably because the pastry was too basic to require instructions, and perhaps also because it was more of a cottage recipe. Tyneham does have one:

DORSET NORFOLK DUMPLINGS

Take a pint and half of flower [1lb], three eggs one white, half a pint of cream a piece of butter as big as an egg, half a pd of Beef suet shred very small, a little nutmeg and salt, mix altogether, when 'tis made, set it before the fir to Rise, when the Water boyls make it up in 3 long Dumplins, half an hour will boyl them, they must be butter'd before they are sent to the Table.

¼lb plain flour	pinch salt
2oz suet	1 egg
½ teaspoon of ground nutmeg	milk to mix (less than ⅛ pint)

Mix all the dry ingredients together with the egg and enough milk to make a stiffish dough. Divide into four or eight dumplings, drop into boiling water (or on top of a stew) and cook for about 20 minutes for the large ones, 15 minutes for the smaller. They grow enormously, and the milk and nutmeg produce an unusual dumpling. The originals must have been enormous, since this quarter recipe will fill the top of a normal saucepan.

This is included in the puddings section of the Tyneham recipe book, but they go well with meat, e.g. with the boiled lamb on p. 63.

Apple Suet Pudding

Bloxworth has a slightly enigmatic pudding from the late eighteenth century which I think must be suet pastry:

TO MAKE AN APPLE PUDDING

Line the pudding-pot with past, the same sort and thickness of that which is put round the little apple puddings which are boil'd in a cloth; fill the pot with apple cut in qrs, make it pretty sweet, and put Lemmon peel or quince to give it a flavour; put a crust upon the top of the pot and apples, and tie it boil for 4 hours or 3 hours and a half according to the size of the Pot. NB it is impossible to have it good, if it does not boil a vast while.

We are not given the recipe for the 'little apple puddings'. Presumably the recipe is for a vast pudding: 2 hours' boiling is plenty for a modern size.

8oz self-raising flour (or plain, adjusted with baking powder)	1½ to 2lb cooking apples, peeled cored and sliced
pinch of salt	3oz sugar
4oz suet	cloves if liked

Mix the flour, salt and suet with enough cold water to make a stiffish paste (about a scant ⅛ pint). Roll out and line a buttered and floured 2-pint pudding basin, keeping some of the pastry to make a lid. Put the apples, mixed with the sugar (with 3 or 4 cloves, if liked) into the lined basin, and cover with the remaining pastry. Steam for 2 hours (see notes on boiled puddings on p. 75).

Apple is probably the best fruit with suet crust, but pears, plums or really any other fruit could be used, adjusting the sugar to taste. Suet crust used to be baked in the oven, but I don't think it turns out so well as when boiled.

Moonshine, or Bread and Butter Pudding

There are two basic versions, baked or boiled. Tyneham has a good baked one:

TO MAKE A MOONSHINE, OR BREAD AND BUTTER PUDDING
When you have well butterd the bottom of your Dish cut some slices of Bread and Butter thick of Butter and thin of Bread. Put a layer of it at the bottom of your dish, then a layer of currants but not too thick, and so on a layer of bread and Butter and a layer of currants till your dish is nearly full, then make a Custard, and pour over it which you must fill up your dish with, put a little Grated Lemon peel in the Custard Three quarters of an Hour will bake it if a Large Pudding.

Custard is given elsewhere in the Tyneham book: see p. 95.

PLAIN PAST CUSTARD
Boil a quart of Cream or new Milk with a Nutmeg cut in pieces and some Cinnamon when its almost cold stirring it all ye while then sweeten it to you tast, put in six eggs well beat leaving out half the eggs mix ym well with the Cream, and strain it into a pan, have ready patty-pans or dishes with puff past put one spoonful of ye Custard in the Bottoms and set them into the oven to bake, when the Crust is hardened fill them up.

Presumably the bit about leaving out the eggs is a mistake for leaving out some of the whites.

About 12oz bread (about 6 good slices), buttered	1½oz sugar (brown is good)
about 4oz currants or sultanas	a little grated nutmeg and cinnamon
1 pint milk	grated zest of a lemon
2–3 eggs	pinch of salt

Butter a dish (use a wide shallow one if you like a crunchy top). Line with bread and butter, strew with currants, cover with more bread and butter, and so on. Mix the milk, eggs, sugar, lemon zest and spices together and pour over the bread. Bake at gas mark 3 for about 50 minutes. The lemon and spices give a good flavour.

Baked Custard

1 pint milk	pinch of salt
2–3 eggs	1 sugar
Either grated zest of a lemon, or a pinch of nutmeg and cinnamon	

Mix all the ingredients together lightly with a fork until there are no 'threads' from the eggs, pour into a buttered dish and bake at gas mark 1 for about an hour; longer will be needed if a ceramic dish is used.

It is only necessary to heat the milk if the custard is to go into pastry cases. If you want to cook the custard in a hotter oven along with other things, place it in a pan of water to come halfway up your dish. This provides a buffer between the heat and the custard. It is also possible to steam the custard.

Very good with fruit pies, or stewed fruit. The spicy custard is best with spiced fruit, lemon with plainer dishes.

The Poor Vicar's Pudding

A boiled version from mid-nineteenth-century Bloxworth:

TO MAKE A BREAD PUDDING (THE POOR VICARS PUDDING)
Take almost half a Pound of Bread Crumb and Crust slice it Thin Boil Milk pour it on the Bread let it stand till thoroughly Soaked then break it very fine add to it a little sugar Six Ounces of Currants three Eggs well Beat four ounces of Beef Suet cut fine a little salt a little grated Nutmeg or orange peel which is best mix it all Well together tye it up Close in a Cloth leaving room for it to rise let the pot boil before it is put in Let the Pudding boil three hours pond Melted Butter on it.

If you put orange in it then Stick it with Orange Peel and put a little Wine in the Butter.

½lb bread, brown or white (about 4 good slices from a large loaf)	pinch salt
½ pint milk	2 eggs
4oz brown sugar	6oz currants
4oz suet	½ teaspoon grated nutmeg
	zest of one or two oranges

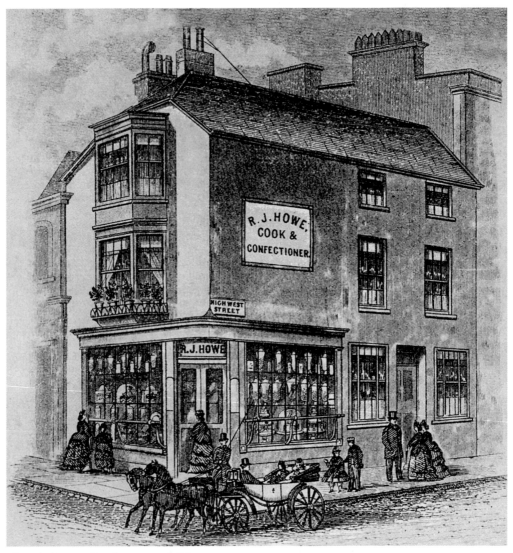

Howe's shop at Dorchester, c. 1860.

Break the bread into pieces in a bowl, boil the milk and pour over. When it has cooled mix with a spoon to smooth it out. Add sugar, suet, salt, eggs, currants, nutmeg and orange zest. Put the mixture into a well-buttered and floured bowl, cover and steam for 2 hours.

The original recipe is a little bland, so I used a little more nutmeg and orange zest. This recipe avoids the tedious task of grating the bread. Another recipe for a brown bread pudding, also from Bloxworth, grates ½lb bread, adds ½lb suet (which seems too much), with ½lb currants, 6oz sugar and a little nutmeg.

Howe's at Dorchester seen in about 1888.

Orange Meringue Pie

ORANGE PUDDING – BLANDFORD, *c.* 1810

Take six ounces of Butter four ounces of Sugar melt them together over a slow fire and keep stirring it all the time then have ready, the yokes of four eggs well beaten and when the butter and Sugar is melted, take it off the fire and stir in the Egg and half a candied orange sliced as thin as possible grate in the peel of a Seville orange and put in the juice of it then beat it a full half hour, roll as thin as a crust as possible to put under and over it.

Better with the whites of the eggs made into meringue on top.

Makes one 8-inch pie

4oz butter	zest and juice one orange
1oz sugar and 3oz sugar	½oz cornflour
3 eggs	pre-cooked pastry case
2oz candied orange peel (the large pieces, sliced, are best)	granulated sugar

---

Melt the butter and 1oz sugar together, whisk the yolks from the eggs, add the melted and cooled butter etc. to the eggs with the finely sliced peel, orange juice and zest and cornflour. Mix well together (if using a liquidiser place all ingredients in, and mix). Pour into a pre-cooked pastry case. Whisk the egg whites until stiff, add 1oz caster sugar. Whisk, add 2oz sugar, stir by hand, put on top of the pie, sprinkle with granulated sugar and cook at gas mark 3 for about 25–35 minutes, until the meringue is just browned. Serve straight from the oven.

The cornflour is only necessary if it is to be served hot, as without it the orange filling can be very runny. It stiffens when cold. A very tasty orange pudding.

Fool

A WHIPED CREAM (TYNEHAM)

Take the Syrrup of any fruit and and mingle with Cream, and sugar to your tast you must whip it with a white whisk till it be thick enough to serve.

We would call this a fool, and would include the whole of the fruit, not just syrup.

For example, 1lb of gooseberries cooked in 2oz butter, then mashed, added to ½ pint whipped cream, with sugar to taste.

Cream and milk in all their forms were popular in the eighteenth century. 'Having ascended thus far [to the first look out, a stone's throw from Weymouth] refresh-

Milk arriving at the butter factory, Dorchester, early 1920s. Factory always seems such an odd name for butter making, but by this time the bulk of butter was mass-produced in 'factories'.

ments may be procured at the Farm house, viz syllabubs, cream and curds, whey butt[er] milk, fruit etc etc'. Weymouth *Guide*, 1791. An early version of cream teas.

Burnt Cream

Today this is known as crème brûlée, but it occurs in Dorset recipe books as burnt cream from the very late seventeenth century. From Mrs Machen's recipe book, Bloxworth:

TO MAKE BURNT CREAM
Take the yolks of four Eggs, one spoonful of flower, a little orange flower water, beat it together, then put in a pint of Cream, and as much Sugar as will sweeten it, stir it together, put in a stick of Cinnamon, and set it on a gentle fire keeping it stirring till tis pretty thick, then pour it in the dish you serve it up in, let it stand till it is as thick

as a Custard, then Sift Duble refin'd Sugar over it, and hold a red hott Sallimander over it till tis burnt pretty Black, serve it up hott.

The salamander was a circular iron plate on a long handle which was heated over the fire, and held over food to cook it. Really it did the job of a modern grill.

either ½ pint single cream	½ tablespoon flour
or ¼ pint each single and double cream	½ tablespoon orange flower water or
2 eggs	pinch of cinnamon (optional)
teaspoon of sugar	sugar, for topping

Heat the cream gently in a thick-bottomed saucepan. Mix the egg yolks, sugar, flour and flavouring (if used). Add the eggy mixture to the cream, and stir together well. Either heat slowly in the saucepan, being careful that it does not boil as it will curdle, stirring the whole time until it thickens, and then pour into fire proof dishes; or heat the mixture together a little and pour into fireproof dishes, place in the oven at gas mark 2 for about 30 minutes in a pan of water, so that the water comes halfway up the dishes. If you are nervous about egg sauces the oven is best.

Having dinner in the Landslip, Lyme Regis, 1842. The huge landslip of 1840 was a popular tourist attraction, and meals could be purchased from a cottage.

When it has cooled sprinkle caster sugar over the top, and place under the grill until it burns. Mrs Machin served it hot but it is usually served cold, when it is very good with fruit.

Some modern recipes suggest heating in a double saucepan, but if you dip your finger in to test the temperature occasionally a thick saucepan is fine. I think a mixture of double and single cream makes it too rich, but others prefer it. Another Dorset recipe uses mace with cinnamon as flavour, and zest of lemon would be good. This amount is enough for three people, as even with single cream it is rich.

Tyneham Pears

TO STEW PEARS

Take a pound of Loaf Sugar a quart of water Juice and Rind of a whole Lemon and Half a Stick of Cinamon Boil these Ingredients in a well Tinn Saucepan a quarter of an Hour Scum it very clean then pare core and quarter four or five Pears put them into your Syrup let them stew gently till they are tender Clear and of a good Colour.

This is in a slightly later hand than the bulk of the Tyneham recipe book, and probably dates from the late eighteenth or early nineteenth century. Warduns (pears) in syrup was a popular medieval dish, presumably because the types of pear available were hard, and so had to be cooked. Red wine and red fruits were used then to dye the pears red in cooking, and a mixture of spices was added.

juice and zest of a lemon	about 1½lb hard pears; Conference
3oz brown sugar	are best
½ teaspoon of ground cinnamon, or	
¼ stick	

Put the lemon zest, juice, sugar and cinnamon in about ¾ pint of water and bring to the boil. Add the peeled, cored and quartered pears and stew gently for about 15 minutes until cooked.

The spice and lemon does not overwhelm the pears, but improves them, and it's a good way to cook apples too. The pears or apples would go well with a baked custard.

Syllabub

Take half a pint of cream a Wine Glass of Sack or sweet Mountain [wine] A White of an egg and sugar to your tast, mix altogether and Whip it with a Wisk or Chocolate Mill, as ye froth rises take it off and lay on a kenge [sieve], when it is drain'd from ye Whey, lay it on your cream.

½ pint whipping cream or double cream

wine glass of sherry, or cider, or white wine

a little orange juice, or lemon zest, or orange flower water (optional)

sugar

Whisk the cream, wine and flavourings together, add sugar to taste, and put into glasses. The 'whey' will separate from the cream overnight if they are kept, but this is not objectionable. Some eighteenth-century syllabubs were coloured with saffron, cochineal or spinach juice, which would look very pretty. This Tyneham recipe suggests 'fill the bottom of your dish with cream and Raspberry jam mix'd well together' and top with this syllabub to produce raspberry trifle.

Sadborow adds lemon juice and a little brandy (no egg) and the instruction 'let it stand all night. When you turn it out the next day it will look like a cheese.'

Sack was a wine-like sweet sherry.

MRS MACHEN'S SILLIBUB

Take a pint of Cream ½ a pint of white wine, ¼ pint of sack the juice of one lemon and the peele sweeten it to your taste mix these together, beat it with a birch rod till the rod will stand upright in them, put them in your sillibub glass; you may keep them some 2 or 3 days before you use them, they will not spoyle without extraordinary hot weather.

This is a more modern type of syllabub, even though the recipe dates from the early eighteenth century.

½ pint double cream
¼ pint white wine
⅛ pint sherry

juice and zest of one lemon
sugar to taste (perhaps 2oz)

Whisk all together, probably with a machine rather than a birch rod.

A rare survivor – from a paper bag of about 1840.

Bread

Abbotsbury, c. 1911, with sacks of flour in the cart.

Bread

Until the early nineteenth century (when potatoes became common) in Dorset bread really was the staff of life, the most important food. The labourers lived on it, and even for the upper classes it was a large element of their diet. In times of shortage and high price or by the very poor, barley meal or beans might be used to make bread, but in the south wheat was the standard for flour, and oats were little used. White flour and white bread was the aim, but until the later nineteenth century absolutely white flour was not possible, so loaves were yellowy at best.

Yeast was obtained from ale barm, the froth which comes to the top when beer is brewed. Households generally made beer and bread, with their own brewing supplying the barm. The bitter taste from the beer had to be washed out of the barm or else the bread would be bitter. Ale barm was temperamental and nothing like so reliable as today's fresh or dried yeast.

Bread was so important that inevitably many superstitions grew up around it. In Dorset it was generally believed that bread baked on Good Friday would never go mouldy, and a tiny loaf made then and preserved through the year would ensure all the bread made being good. It was used, grated, as a medicine for cows and people. On a rather more pagan note, crosses were made in the flour when the dough was left to rise overnight, to prevent its being bewitched.

Loaves in the past were much larger: from 1709 the standard sizes were the quartern, or quarter peck loaf weighing about 4½lb, the half peck at double that, and the enormous peck loaf, 17½lb. Even the smallest, the eighth peck loaf, was larger than today's large loaf of 28oz. The towns had bakeries from medieval times, but in the country those who had bread ovens used them to bake a weekly batch of bread. (Presumably the large number of bread pudding recipes comes from the need to cheer up stale bread at the end of the week.)

Even small villages had bakehouses by the late nineteenth century; the 1895 *Directory* for Dorset gives about 150 villages with bakers and more than 300 bakers in the county. Even somewhere as small as Tarrant Monkton (219 people) had a baker, and Corfe Castle had 6, some of whom doubled as shopkeepers. Many were alongside mills where the flour was ground. W.S. Joyce wrote about his father's bakehouse at White Mill, Shapwick in the 1890s where the mill, bakehouse and farm were all run together. It was a big bakehouse with three men baking. There was one large oven:

A stout iron door closed its mouth and inside was a deep and low cavern paved with flat stones. It was heated chiefly with faggots of furze cut on the downs and kept in stacks on the spare ground between the mill and the river. When the faggots had burnt themselves out, the door of the oven was opened and any embers that remained were raked out by means of a long-handled iron tool, curved at the end into a half circle. A second implement was used to clear out the small embers still remaining in the oven and to cool the floor slightly. This consisted of a long pole which was attached to a short length of chain and a piece of sacking. The sacking was dipped in water and then pushed and turned about over the floor of the oven until every glowing cinder had been 'douted' and swept out. The oven was now ready to receive the batch of loaves.

The dough had been made and put to rise first thing in the morning. When removed from the bin, the dough was placed on the lid of the next bin and kneaded. As the kneading proceeded lumps of dough were torn off and flung upon the scales, and it was surprising how frequently an experienced man could remove exactly the amount to make a loaf. This lump was again torn apart, the largest portion remaining under the left hand. After further kneading, the smaller right hand portion was put on top of the larger left hand lump and a final dig given with the knuckles to produce the depression always found in the centre of the top of a cottage loaf. Loaves were made in two sizes and, when I first knew anything about the bakehouse, only cottage loaves were produced there; loaves baked in tins came into fashion considerably later.

The loaves were introduced into the oven by means of long-handed wooden spades known as peels, and were removed by the same means.

Cakes went into the oven after the bread had been removed; they required a gradually declining heat. Our own pies were often baked in the bakehouse oven; but I never remember seeing a joint of any kind cooked in it and was rather surprised, when I went to live in Somerset, to find that it was a common practice in the villages to have joints cooked at the local bakehouse.

In the nineteenth century labourers in Dorset were commonly paid partly in corn, in quantity ranging from one to three bushels a week, and often of poor quality, 'tailing' or small corn. Mrs Bustle, wife of a farm labourer from Whitchurch giving evidence to an inquiry in 1843, thought tailing corn made good bread: 'The bread we make at home is better than baker's bread: I make six loaves out of a bushel of corn [i.e. the finished loaves weighed about 10–12lb each] we have not quite as much as that every week; but what we have, with a bag of potatoes [240lb], is quite as much as we consume at home. Four baker's loaves, with the potatoes, are not enough. Baker's bread does not satisfy the children; it is licked away in no time, and they are hungry all day long with it.' Mrs Bustle was feeding two adults and five children aged 12 downwards on these massive loaves.

Interest in wholemeal, stoneground flour started in the later nineteenth century, and in 1909 James Foot was advertising in the *Dorset County Chronicle* '"The Staff of Life", at Last – if you want to see upon your table once more the GOOD OLD-FASHIONED LOAF OF BREAD nourishing to nerves, bone and brain . . . try FOOT'S PURE STONE-MADE FLOUR' etc. Sounds very modern. By 1911 he was adding 'beware of Spurious Imitations'.

Moore's bread cart, c. 1900. (Moore's collection)

Brown Bread

2lb '81%' brown flour	2 teaspoons salt
½oz fresh yeast or packet dried yeast	3 tablespoons olive oil or similar
(see p. 34 for using yeast)	

Start the yeast if necessary, mix all ingredients with enough warm water to make a stiff dough (probably about ¾ pint, but it varies depending on the flour). Knead thoroughly, half fill a large bread tin and use the little left over for rolls, or half fill two small bread tins. Leave in a warm place for a couple of hours for it to grow, then bake at gas mark 7, reducing the temperature after half an hour to gas mark 5, for about 45 minutes in all for small loaves, 30 minutes or less for rolls, perhaps 50 minutes for a large loaf.

Flour that is 81 per cent wholemeal makes good brown bread, and is much easier than 100%. The result is probably similar to wheat loaves made before the middle of the nineteenth century. Brown bread needs only one rising, white two (see below) – health food shops in the county, and several mills, sell ground locally grown wheat, and although the varieties grown have changed, earlier cooks would have used local corn.

Moore's bread cart in 1912, delivering to the villages. (Moore's collection)

White Bread

1½lb strong white flour, sometimes called bread flour	packet dried yeast or ½oz fresh yeast
	2 teaspoons salt
	¾ pint warm water
(see p. 34 for using yeast)	

(see p. 34 for using yeast)

Start the yeast if necessary, then mix all the ingredients together to form a stiffish dough. Form into a ball, cover with a plastic bag and put in a warm place for 1½–2 hours. It will double in size. Then knead the dough by hand or machine for a couple of minutes, halve and place each half in a well-oiled tin and put it back in the warm place until it doubles in size, probably about 45 minutes. Bake at gas mark 8 for about 30 minutes. When done the loaves will sound hollow when knocked on the base.

This makes two smallish loaves: a tin 8-inch × 4 × 2½-inch deep is ideal as the second rising will just fill it, and the loaf will grow more on top in the over. one ounce of sugar, two ounces of currants or sultanas and some ground spice (cinnamon, nutmeg, mace or any mixture) added to half the dough makes a nice currant loaf, and can be cooked in an 8-inch cake tin.

Barley and Wheat Bread

Barley bread was eaten by the labourers of Dorset in the eighteenth century, and barley flour was used in poor areas in the nineteenth century. As recollected at Ashmore, 'bread was very dear, so they used to eat barley cake. My grandmother would buy barley meal which was cheaper than barley flour. She would put it through a range [sieve] to get the flour out to make the cakes and they would eat them with treacle or blue cheese. . . . At Marnhull the bannock or barley cake was baked in a round crock hung over the fire' (*Dorset Up Along and Down Along*, 1935).

Bread made from barley flour alone and raised with yeast is disgusting, looking bad with a heavy crumbly texture and a bitter taste, but a barley flour mixed with wheat flour makes a good loaf, with an unusual flavour:

12oz strong white flour, or 81% wholemeal	2 teaspoons salt
	¾ pint warm water
8oz barley flour	½oz fresh or packet dried yeast

Make as white bread.

Outdoor tea gardens were popular from the later nineteenth century. Harry Smith's tea gardens were right in the middle of Lyme, but look very rural here in about 1911. The notice outside says 'To the gardens'. (Lyme Regis Museum)

Broad Street, Lyme Regis. (Lyme Regis Museum)

Mrs Machen's French Bread

TO MAKE FRENCE BREAD

Take a quarter of a peck of flower [just over 3lb], six whites of eggs beat to a froth, one pint of small bear yeast, boyl the milk and let it stand till tis blood warm, mix to the stiffness of a Pudding, let it rise, one hour will bake it.

This later addition to Mrs Machen's recipe book is probably mid-eighteenth century. There are two difficulties: the quantity of milk is not stated, and nor is the type of pudding. Presumably it is meant to be wetter than normal bread, or else the consistency would not be specified.

½oz fresh or packet dried yeast	pinch of salt
3 egg whites	½ pint of water
1½lb strong white flour	¼ pint milk

Start the yeast, if necessary. Whisk the egg whites until stiff. Add ½ pint of warm water and ¼ pint milk, then the flour. Knead until well mixed together. It should be wetter than normal bread dough. Leave to rise for about 1½ hours, when it will have doubled in size. Put into bread tins, or form into rolls, and bake at gas mark 6 for about 30 minutes for large rolls, 45 minutes for loaves.

This makes good crusty rolls, crisp outside with a soft rich inside. The uncooked dough is the stickiest imaginable.

Milk Loaf

WHITE FRENCH BREAD

To four pound of flower take a quart of new milk and three spoonsfulls of ale yeast not bitter a quarter of an ounce of salt if the weather be warm you must not make the milk to hot but if cold then very warm let the dough lie till tis full roof then make em up into Roles about half a pound weight and just when they begin to crack on the top put em into a quick oven and stand an hour to bake.

These proportions are the same as those given for ordinary white bread above, but replacing the water with milk. It makes a rather more crusty loaf than when mixed with water, but not so crusty as Mrs Machen's other recipe for French Bread.

Stooking the corn: an illustration for Tess *by Vivien Gribble, 1926.*

*The milking team
at Barton Farm,
Cerne Abbas,
c. 1910.*

Ingredients and method as white bread, but use ¾ pint milk in place of the water. If using a yeast which needs 'starting' use ¼ pint of water for that, and only ½ pint milk. Bake at gas mark 6.

Apple Bread

Apples seem to have been added to bread as well as cakes.

1½lb cooking apples	1½lb strong white flour
½oz fresh or packet dried yeast	pinch of salt

Peel, core and chop the cooking apples. Cook in as little water as possible and allow to cool. (Start yeast, if necessary.) Mash the apples, and mix them with the flour and yeast. If the dough is not wet enough, add a little water, but usually the apples add enough moisture. Knead. Put to rise in a warm place for a couple of hours. Half fill bread tins, and let it rise again for about 20 minutes. Bake at gas mark 7 for about 40 minutes, reducing the temperature if it seems to be getting too brown.

The apple darkens the bread, which has a good crisp crust, and alters the texture, but it does not taste at all strongly which is a disappointment.

Chopped apple added to the dough before the second proving gives more apple flavour. About 6oz finely chopped uncooked apple to 1lb dough is best, and it should be used for rolls.

111

Carrying the harvest in Dorset in the 1890s. Good hats.

Milking in the yard at Horn Dairy, Beaminster, with a visitor looking on, 1909.

Cakes and Biscuits

Making Dorset knobs at Moore's Bakery, Morecombelake, 1928. (Moore's collection)

Cakes and Biscuits

Before baking powders were marketed in the 1860s cakes were raised either by beating the eggs for up to an hour, or by means of yeast. Dorset has several traditional recipes for yeast cakes, and there must have been many more which do not survive. All are similar, but vary in the amount and type of spice and fruit used. Everyday recipes have less butter, and seventeenth-century ones include rose water, but often no eggs.

The yeast cakes are well worth making: soft, rich and, despite the low quantities of sugar, sweet. They are easier to make than 'modern' cakes, but take longer because of the rising time. Fresh or dried yeast is much more reliable than the ale barm originally used, and the mixture is very adaptable and good-tempered. Most of the eighteenth-century recipes are for large quantities, and one wonders how the cake was ever cooked through without the edges burning.

Tyneham Yeast Cake

Tyneham's eighteenth-century yeast cake is full of spice and fruit:

TO MAKE A PLUM CAKE
5 pound of flower dried 6 pd of Currants wash'd and dryed, a pd of Raisins stoned and shred small, half a pd of Citron 20 eggs half the whites 3 doz of cloves 2 nutmegs 6 blades of Mace and as much Cinnamon a pd of sweet Almonds Blanch'd and beat well, half a pd of sugar, two pd and half of Butter a pint and half of Cream, half a pint of sack, and a pint of new Ale yeast.

Pouring coffee at Winterbourn St Martins, 1872.

NB YE MANNER TO MAKE IT UP

Strew in your spice and sugar first, warm the Butter and Cream blood warm till the butter is melted, beat yr Eggs and mix them with ye sack and yeast, then strain it tho' a sive into yr Cream and Butter: make it into a thin batter in ye Middle of your flower, ye Almonds and Raisins put in next, and strew the rest of the flower lightly over; mix up whilst oven is heating, and let it stand by the fire to rise, then take it up and put in your Currants as quick as you can, for much handling makes it heavy let your oven be ready before you mix it, if you think it too hot cold it [the oven] with water: two hours bakes it.

For Two Cakes

2lb strong white flour	¾ pint of milk, or replace a little of the
packet dried yeast, or ½oz fresh	milk with sweet sherry (sack)
¼ teaspoon each ground nutmeg,	1lb margarine or butter
cloves, mace and cinnamon (or even	3 eggs
more if you like spice)	1½lb currants, or a mixture of fruit
pinch of salt	2oz peel
3oz sugar (I have used brown or white,	4oz ground almonds (optional)
both successful)	

I don't think it's worth using butter unless you leave all or most of the spice out. A plainer spiceless version with only half the fruit is very buttery, a totally different cake.

Follow instructions to start your yeast if necessary. Put flour, yeast, spices, salt, sugar in a bowl. Warm the milk and melt the butter or margarine (cut into small lumps) in it. Let the milk cool to blood heat (hotter will kill the yeast) then add it to the flour etc. Add the eggs (no need to beat them). Mix together, don't knead it at any stage. The result should be wetter-looking than bread dough, but not like cake mixture. Leave to rise, covered by a plastic bag in the airing cupboard or other warm place for about 1½ hours. Mix the fruit in. Divide between two well-buttered 8-inch tins (deep – it will double in size in the oven), return to warm place and allow to rise for half an hour. Bake at gas mark 5 for about 45 minutes to an hour, longer if it has grown a lot: like bread it should sound hollow when knocked on the bottom, and like cake a skewer should come out clean. It is very good-tempered about being returned to the oven if underdone.

A single cake may be made by halving the quantities, but two are as easy to make as one, and they freeze well. Eight ounces of chopped fresh apricots are a good addition.

Sadborow has plainer cakes – 2lb flour to only ½lb butter but ½lb sugar for 'A Good Common Cake'. 'Common Cake' from the same book is plainer yet – 1½lb flour to ¼lb butter, four eggs, ¼lb sugar.

Portland Dough Cake

All the recipes for this were recorded in the twentieth century, and I do wonder if originally it was a yeast cake like the Tyneham recipes. Certainly all are agreed that it varied considerably from family to family but all the twentieth-century recipes start from bread dough. This was contributed to the *Dorset Magazine* in 1969.

2lb bread dough	¼lb brown sugar
1½lb currants	¼lb mixed peel
1lb lard (with additionally ¼lb butter for a richer cake)	1 teaspoon nutmeg
See p. 35 for using yeast	

The bread dough of the recipe is presumably proved once, then all the ingredients mixed together. It is easier to add the fat if it has been melted and allowed to cool. Prove for about 30 minutes, divide into two cakes allowing room in the tins for it to grow in the oven, and bake at gas mark 6 for about 30 minutes.

If making alone, rather than as a by-product of bread making, it would be easier to melt the fat in the water (or milk) used to make the bread, and then add all the other ingredients after the second proving.

Another recipe substitutes gooseberries for the dried fruit, but add more sugar.

Blandford Dough Cake

This type of dough cake is found in the recipe book of about 1810 from Blandford:

TO MAKE A GOOD BUN
Take three pound and a half of Dough the same that Roles are made of – one pound of Butter dissolved by a slow fire till it is like cream, 8 eggs well beat, mix these well together, then add one pound of powder sugar, a large nutmeg gratered or any spice you please, and two pound of currants when they are well beaten together let it stand an hour rise – It will take three hours baking – If you chuse to enrich it, add a quarter of a pound of blanched Almonds and the same quantity of Candid orange and Lemon peel.

Roll dough was usually enriched with butter, which seems unlikely here as more butter is added. There is no recipe for rolls in the book, but perhaps the dough was made with milk rather than water. The original bun must have been huge, presumably cooked without a tin.

The child disrupts tea at Winterbourn St Martins, 1872.

1½lb bread dough made with milk	8oz sugar
½lb butter	½ nutmeg grated
4 eggs	1lb currants
	2oz candied peel
(see p. 34 for using yeast)	

Melt the butter, allow to cool and whisk with the eggs. Mix all ingredients together, divide between two cake tins and put in a warm place to prove for about half an hour. Bake at gas mark 6 for about 30 minutes.

This has a lot more sugar than the Tyneham yeast cake, but is otherwise very similar, apart from the sequence of putting the ingredients together.

Sherborne Stodger

This elegantly named bun has recently been revived by a Sherborne baker. Traditionally it was a yeast-raised dough, with equal quantities of butter, sugar, and flour and some eggs. This is clearly a celebration dough cake, very high in sugar and fat. Best purchased.

Dorset Apple Cake

Difficult to find an authentic early recipe for this, although it is always considered traditionally Dorset. None of the eighteenth-century manuscript cookery books have it, although they include many cakes. Apples (and most other fruits) were then reduced to a sieved pulp before being added to puddings, so that the recipe used today with chunks of apple seems unlikely to be early.

Today there must be nearly as many apple cake recipes as there are people who make them. Most seem to agree that a rubbing-in method should be used, but the amount, or even presence, of spices varies wildly. Almost all agreed that cooking apples should be used, but not whether currants etc. should be added.

Apple cake was voted Dorset's National Dish at Dorset Food Week 2006 and the winning cake had sliced apple beautifully arranged on the top like a French tart.

A very simple recipe from Marnhull, recorded in 1940 but then believed to date from the 1860s, gives a ½lb flour, ¼lb lard, 2 good-sized apples chopped up very fine, and 2oz sugar, all mixed with a little milk and baked in the oven on a greased plate. The lack of spices, eggs or butter suggests that it is a cottage recipe rather than one from a richer kitchen. William Barnes's poem of 1835 'Father Come Home' includes a similar cake, cooked either on a hearthstone or a sheet of iron over the fire:

> Your supper's nearly ready. I've a-got
> Some teäties here a-doen in the pot;
> I wish wi' all my heart I had some meat.
> I got a little ceäke too, here, a-beäken o'n
> Upon the vier. 'Tis done by this time though
> He's nice an' moist; vor when I were-a meäkin o'n
> I stuck some bits ov apple in the dough.

Paul Nash was fed apple cake in a hotel in Purbeck while he was writing the Shell *Guide* (1936), and found it 'discouraging . . . neither nice or digestible. . . . In the hands of a good cook it might turn out rather like a sponge apple sandwich, if that can be imagined.' He must have been offered a version which contained no fruit but apple, similar to one recorded from North Chideock in about 1932:

¼lb butter	¼lb sugar
½lb plain flour	½lb cooking apples, pared, cored and
pinch salt	chopped
1½ teaspoons baking powder	(or ½lb gooseberries, topped and tailed)
	milk to mix (less than ¼ pint)

Rub the butter into the flour, salt and baking powder. Add the sugar and chopped apples, then mix to a thick paste with milk. Put into a cake tin and bake at gas mark 4 for 45–60 minutes: a skewer should come clean from the cake when done.

This is enough for one 8-inch tin. More apples could be added. The cake is soft and plain, with a good buttery taste. The recipe was recorded for *Good Things in England* (1932) along with the method of serving: it was eaten 'hot or cold with butter or cream. Also I am told they make it with gooseberries instead of apple. Some put in currants, but I think it is nicest as a tea cake, and it heats up well the next day.' The cake is fine on its own, even the next day without reheating. Blackcurrants or gooseberries can also be used, but the basic cake mixture needs to have, say, 2oz extra sugar to make up for the tartness of the fruit. Small squares of rhubarb are good as well.

Spicy Dorset Apple Cake

4oz butter or margarine	4oz caster or brown sugar
8oz flour, self raising or adjusted	1lb cooking apples
1½ teaspoons mixed spice, or a	3oz currants or sultanas
mixture to your taste	2 eggs

Rub the margarine and the flour together, add the spices, sugar, peeled, cored and sliced apples, currants and the beaten eggs. Put the mixture in a large cake tin (10-inch round or 8-inch square) and bake at gas mark 6 for 35–45 minutes. The large amount of apple makes the cake a little fragile, so leave in the tin for 5 minutes or more before removing. If you do not have a large cake tin, use two smaller cake tins and reduce the cooking time a little.

Chopped apple can be added to virtually any cake: it is good in smaller quantities and finely chopped (say ¼–½lb per cake) in a fruit cake.

Farmer's Loaf from the 1917 manuscript cookery book is another version of apple cake, using golden syrup (on the market from about 1880). The original is 1lb apples; 4oz margarine; 1 egg; 6oz currants; 1lb flour; teaspoon biccarbonate of soda; powdered cinnamon; teacup golden syrup; spoonful of milk or more if needed. Fat rubbed into flour, add all dry ingredients and cooked apples, mix in well beaten egg and golden syrup. Bake in flat greased tin for one hour.

This makes a large cake, looking like a loaf, or a very large rock cake, but doughier and softer. Pre-cooking the apples is unnecessary and makes them wetter and more difficult to use.

Farmer's Loaf

4oz margarine	1lb cooking apples, peeled, cored
1lb self-raising flour	and chopped
2 eggs	6oz golden syrup
	6oz currants
	pinch of powdered cinnamon

Rub the margarine into the flour, add well-beaten eggs, then rest of ingredients and mix well (the worst thing about golden syrup is measuring it – coat the bottom of the weighing pan with flour first). If using a machine add the apples after rubbing in and the machine will chop them. They can be reduced to fine pieces if you like. The mixture is fairly wet. This amount will make a loaf tin or two deepish 8-inch cake tins, or one 8-inch tin and some little cakes. Bake at Mark 3½ for about 45 minutes for the large tin, 25–30 minutes for small cakes, 1 hour 20 minutes for loaf tin. When done a skewer comes out clean from the middle of the cake, which will have shrunk a little from the sides of the tin. Extract carefully, and cool on a tray.

This is an unusual cake, perhaps a bit puddingy, but worth making. Different dried fruits could be added, and different spices.

Tea Cake

A small group of recipes for cakes made with lard or dripping survives in Dorset. One from Piddletrenthide, called Railway Pudding, dates from the 1850s and is very similar to another Thomas Hardy's cook made as Yeovil tea cake: '1lb flour, 6oz dripping, 4oz sugar, 1 egg, a little lemon peel, milk. Mix with a little milk and bake on a dinner-plate. Eat hot.' Portland Heavy Cake has more lard and sugar: 1lb flour; 8oz lard; 7oz sugar; 1lb currants, fat rubbed in to the flour and mixed with water (*Dorset Year Book*, 2003).

3oz dripping or lard	½lb flour, preferably wholemeal or
2oz caster sugar	half wholemeal
1 egg	teaspoon baking powder
	¼ pint milk
	peel, or currants, sultanas etc.

Mix the dripping and sugar together (easier if the dripping is at room temperature) add the egg; mix. Mix in the flour, baking powder and milk, peel and dried fruit. The result will be a very stiff mixture. Put into an 8-inch cake tin, and bake at gas mark 4 for 40–50 minutes.

Best with wholemeal flour, and improved by the addition of dried fruit. Doubtless lard or dripping was commonly used in cottage cakes, because it was so much cheaper than butter. Surprisingly the dripping does not taste strongly in the finished cake.

Medieval gingerbread was breadcrumbs with lots of spice and honey, but from the later seventeenth century black treacle was the main flavouring, along with spices. Some recipes, like the early nineteenth-century Sadborow one below, leave out the ginger.

Taking tea in Dorchester, 1890s.

SADBOROW GINGERBREAD CAKES

Take 3lb flour, 1lb of sugar, 1lb of butter rubbed in very fine; a large nutmeg grated then take 1lb of treacle and a ¼ pint of cream make them warm together and make up the bread stiff roll it out and then cut it with a glass or tea cup or small glasses or make them round like nuts. Bake them on tin plates in a slack oven.

1lb flour	2 spoonfuls cream
5oz sugar	teaspoon ground nutmeg
5oz butter	(optional: teaspoon ground ginger)
5oz treacle	

Measuring treacle is awful – either simply take ⅓ of a one-pound tin or 2 very sticky large spoonfuls. If using a mixer simply whizz all ingredients together – the result is soft but not wet. Roll out and cut into rounds, or simply form by hand into rounds 'like nuts'. Bake on a well-buttered tray at gas mark 3 for 20–30 minutes – good soft or crisp, with or without ginger.

This is a much gentler version than the Tyneham one.

121

Spicy Gingerbread

GINGER-BREAD, MRS TEELD
A Pd of Flour ½ a pd of Treacle a quar of a pd of Sugar a quar of a pd of Butter one Egg ½ an oz of ginger grated ¼ an oz of Carriway seeds ¼ an oz of Coriander Seeds.

This Tyneham recipe is typical of several eighteenth-century ones in Dorset recipe books. Some replace the egg with a little milk.

1 egg	¼lb soft margarine
¼lb sugar	2½ teaspoons each of ground ginger,
½lb black treacle	ground coriander and caraway seeds
	1lb flour

Whisk the egg, add the sugar, treacle, margarine and spices, then the flour. It will make a stiff paste. Put into a flat pan, well buttered and floured, and cook at gas mark 3 for about 30 minutes. This will leave the gingerbread softish. To crisp it right through cook for another 15 minutes. Alternatively roll out and cut thin biscuits, or make gingerbread men. The mixture keeps its shape very well.

Very spicy, but delicious: it bites back. Margarine serves just as well as butter, as the spices are too strong for the taste of butter to come through. It could be made with half quantities of spice, but most people seem to like the original. It would make a good pudding with a plain cold custard.

Mrs Freke's Almond Biscuits

MRS FREKES ALMOND BISKETS [MRS MACHEN]
Grate three lemons into a pound of powder sugar, half a pound of almonds pounded, six eggs all beaten together with a quarter of a pound of flour. Bake them in patty pans and sift loaf sugar over them. Let em be beaten an hour.

[another hand] Lady B' [unreadable] has only two lemons, nine eggs ¾lb almonds a spoonful of orange flower water. Mrs Freks the best receipt.

The identical recipe is found at Tyneham, so these biscuits were obviously popular.

¼lb chopped almonds	2oz plain flour
zest ½ lemon	2oz caster sugar
2 small eggs	

A tiny fair at Lyme Regis, 1890s. This spot was where the gingerbread sellers had their stalls. (Lyme Regis Museum)

If using whole almonds blanch them and put in liquidiser with lemon peel and eggs. Liquidise to leave the nuts in small pieces, add the flour and mix. If using chopped almonds mix together with the beaten eggs, zest and flour. I prefer the sugar sprinkled on the top of the mixture, but it could be added into it. Put the mixture on a buttered and floured baking tray, or roll out and cut with fancy cutters (they can be quite small, as they are rich) and then place on baking tray. Cook at gas mark 4 for 20–25 minutes.

The end result will be yellow, both nutty and lemony. Sophisticated biscuits, good with coffee after dinner or with custards or syllabub. The mixture of nuts and lemon is common in eighteenth-century recipes.

Cranborne Biscuits

A RECEIPT TO MAKE BISKETS LIKE THOSE AT CRANBOURN [MRS MACHEN, 1709]
Rub an ounce of Butter into a pound of Flour, put the yolk of an Egg, a spoonful of fine sugar, and a spoonful of Yeast into as much warm Milk as will mix the Flour; Let it lye to rise an Hour, cut it out without rolling it, and let it lye by the Fire till put

into the oven. Reserve a little milk and yolk of Egg to do over the Biskets with a feather. They are very good if cut long about the size of Naples Biskets.

packet of dried yeast or ½oz fresh	scant ½ pint milk
3oz butter	1 egg
1½lb white flour	optional flavourings: lemon or
1½oz caster sugar	orange zest, orange flower water,
	cinnamon, mace, caraway seeds

Start yeast if necessary. Rub the butter into the flour, add the sugar and yeast. Heat the milk a little and add to the flour along with the egg. Put in a warm place for an hour to rise. Then add flavouring, using, say, about 1 tablespoon of orange flower water with the zest of an orange to one-third of the mixture; ½ a teaspoon of mace and another of cinnamon to another third, and caraway seeds in the last. Although Mrs Machen says not to roll it out, it is possible to do so, and then use cutters to make pretty shapes. Naples biscuits were finger-shaped, but flattened circles look prettier. Put the biscuits on metal trays, allowing room for them to rise, and return to a warm place for half an hour. Brush the tops with milk and egg yolk, or just milk. Bake at gas mark 6 for 15–25 minutes, depending on the size of the biscuits. They are good just browned outside, or brown all through.

These grow enormously in the oven, and are slightly scone-like. If made finger-shaped they look like little rolls. Good as biscuits, or with syllabub or custard.

Dorset Knobs

The first visitor to record these Dorset specialities was Paul Nash in the 1930s: '*Dorset Knobs are very light rusks abut the size and shape of golf balls, with the resilience of a ship's biscuit. They go very well with Blue Vinny cheese.*' In the '30s there were still several bakeries producing them, but now there is only one, Moore's of Morecombelake. There they are still made by hand from the traditional recipe, a particular flour, yeast, fat and sugar mixture very similar to that for Cranborne biscuits, but with water instead of milk. The tiny circular rolls are shaped by hand, baked at a high temperature, then turned so the bases cook and finally completely dried through at a very low temperature for up to 3½ hours. The result is very durable: if sealed in a tin or similar they will keep nearly indefinitely.

Knobs seem to have been particularly popular in west Dorset and remained a local delicacy, not being mentioned by any of the guide writers or travellers before the 1930s. Amazingly they did not figure in the Society of Dorset Men's London Dinner until the 1920s, although from 1904 blue vinney cheese was served. Since the 1930s they have become a gourmet food, sold in shops far afield.

An advertisement for Moore's Dorset biscuits.
(Moore's collection)

Traditionally knobs were served with blue vinney cheese, or eaten for breakfast soaked in tea to make them soft. The name is thought to come from the High Top or Dorset knob button, a pointed conical form of the hand-made buttons made in Dorset during the eighteenth and first half of the nineteenth centuries. Knobs are the direct descendant of the medieval biscuit, bread which was sliced and then dried out completely in a slow oven. The word biscuit means twice cooked, and the double-cooked bread was very durable, suitable for taking on journeys, or for soldiers' rations. Ship's biscuit is another version, and seventeenth-century cookery books have recipes for biskets or bisket bread made with eggs, flour, sugar and spices which were baked and then dried out in just the same way.

Dorset knobs were certainly being made in the middle of the nineteenth century by the Moores, and in 1880 the bakery at Morcombelake was established, producing bread and cakes as well as Dorset knobs. After the Second World War bread production stopped, and that of knob and biscuits increased. Today, as well as knobs, many types of superlative sweet biscuits are made from traditional ingredients. The bakery can be visited to see them being made, and there is a shop selling the knobs, biscuits and other Dorset foods.

Dorset Wiggs

Dorset knobs should be bought, not made, as they are difficult, but 'wiggs' a descendant of the medieval enriched breads, are worth making. They were popular in the eighteenth century for breakfast. How they got their name is uncertain but some versions were triangular and so looked like eighteenth-century wigs. Mrs Bond's recipe from Tyneham is easy.

Take 4 pd of fflower warm, then take a quart of new Milk warm and a pint of Ale yeast not bitter Wet the flower with it, and Lay it before the fire to rise when the Oven is hot put into it with yr hands one pd of butter half a pd of sugar and 4oz caraway seeds strew'd in by degrees and bake ym on Tin plates in a quick Oven.

½oz fresh yeast or packet dried yeast	pinch of salt
½ pint of milk	¼lb butter
¼ pint water	2oz sugar
1lb strong white flour	1oz caraway seeds (optional)
(see p. 34 for using yeast)	

Start the yeast if necessary in ¼ pint warm water. Warm the milk a little, and add the milk and water to the flour and salt. Mix thoroughly. Put in a warm place to rise for a couple of hours. Melt the butter, allow to cool until just warm and add to the dough along with the sugar and caraway seeds, if used. (Other spices could be added.) Pour the sloppy mixture into cake tins (about four: larger shallow rectangular tins can be used) to a depth of about ¼–¾ of an inch. Put in a warm place to rise for about 20 minutes, and then bake at gas mark 7 for about 30–40 minutes.

Candlemas fair in Dorchester in 1910. Special cakes and biscuits were sold at these seasonal fairs.

Corn stooked to dry after cutting, probably 1870s.

Moreton Wiggs

Judith Frampton's recipe of 1708, used at Moreton House, can be cooked without an enclosing tin.

½oz fresh yeast or packet dried yeast	1lb strong white flour
⅓ pint milk	teaspoon caraway seeds
1lb butter	pinch ground cloves, mace and
1 egg	nutmeg
2oz sugar	pinch salt

Start the yeast if necessary in ⅛ pint of water (see p. 34), and deduct that amount from the milk. Warm the milk, and melt the butter in it. Beat the egg, and as soon as the milk and butter is cool mix all ingredients together. Put in a warm place to rise for a couple of hours. Form into 3 or 4 large flat buns, return to warm place to rise for about 20 minutes, then bake at gas mark 6 for 25–35 minutes.

The Dorchester butter factory, the destination for much Dorset milk, 1920s.

Mr W. Oliver carrying the milk at Netherbury in 1949.

Preserved Fruit

*The original title page for an early
cookery book. They usually had many
recipes for preserving fruit, as this one
does.*

Preserved Fruit

Sugar, vital for fruit preserving, was imported in tiny quantities from the medieval period, but it was not generally used until the seventeenth century. Even then it was very expensive, and so restricted to the upper classes. One Dorset family was very successfully involved in growing and importing sugar. Azariah Pinney (1661–1719) of Bettiscombe, west Dorset, was exiled to the West Indies for his part in the Monmouth rebellion of 1685, and became a sugar plantation owner. This was the time of huge expansion in sugar production, and he laid the foundations of a great fortune.

Seventeenth- and early eighteenth-century recipe books are full of instructions for fruit preserves, most of them solid cakes of fruit and sugar which were stored wrapped in paper rather than jars. Mrs Machen's recipe book has a fabulous 'cake' consisting of dried fruits stuck together with sugar, covered with white icing, and then covered with leaf gold. All the dried fruits were display food, demonstrating both skill and prosperity, and that 'cake' must have been the culmination. Preserves were usually served as the dessert course, and were often given as presents. In 1616 Weymouth Corporation sent Mrs Pynne '6lb 1 qt of painted marmalady in a fayre boxe at 18*d* p lb and 3lb of conserves of pottatta at 18*d* p lb'. Marmalade at this date meant a preserve of quinces, and may have been imported. Painted is difficult to interpret, but could mean it contained gold. Potatoes had only been known in England for fifty years when this present was made and they were used in sweet recipes well into the eighteenth century. (Both marmalade and potatoes were widely regarded as aphrodisiacs in the sixteenth and seventeenth centuries: Mrs Pynne's relationship with Weymouth Corporation sounds interesting.)

The gift was both stylish and costly: for comparison two years later three Weymouth men supplied a pirate vessel as it 'appered unto Mr Mayor by all conjectural likelyhoode' with 'a quarter of mutton, a pound of butter and four or five gallons of beer'. All this cost just 4*s*, less than a third of the cost of the 9lb of preserves.

From the later nineteenth century jam was produced commercially and locally; Cornick's, grocers at Bridport, made jam from the 1890s. Their advertising sounds very modern: in 1913 they extolled Cornick's New Season marmalade 'made from Seville oranges and refined sugar only, and contains no Chemical Preservative or Colouring Matter; therefore it possesses all the valuable tonic properties for which the Seville orange is so famous. This Marmalade is the finest possible to produce, and is manufactured in Bridport, SUPPORT LOCAL INDUSTRY and HELP the PROSPERITY of YOUR OWN TOWN.' Sounds like the local food movement of the twenty-first century, except that the oranges were imported. Many of their other preserves were made from fruit from their own land, and when a reporter visited in July 1948 he was impressed by the girls picking gooseberries. 'They presented a lovely picture as they came in from the garden carrying baskets of fresh juicy fruit', which was immediately made into jam. This was still rationed in 1948: Cornick's could produce the month's ration for a town the size of Bridport in one day – 5,000lb.

One Dorset recipe book of about 1640 contains only recipes for fruit. Joan Turbeville's preserves are different from our jam only because she cooked them for so long that they formed a solid cake. Most of her fruits could have been home grown – apricots, peaches, quinces, plums, cherries, raspberries, apples and pears – but the oranges and lemons were certainly imported and expensive.

'Pippinge paste' is a typical example: 'first peare your pippings and coare them and put them into a thinn sugar A pownde of pippings put a pownde of sugar and boyle it together and as it boyleth tacke of the froth of it and stir it as it boyleth that it may not burn to, and lett it boyle while it is verry thicke before you tacke it of the fiare and when it is cowld lay it out to your own fancey.'

A slight variant of this recipe (called gateaux de pomme) was used at Tyneham from the eighteenth century to the twentieth: 2lb of apple pulp (cooked for several hours to reduce it down) to 1½lb sugar, with addition of a lemon rind (presumably grated). It was stored in handleless tea-bowls.

Apple Jam

sharp, tasty cooking apples	1lb of sugar (preserving sugar is best)
zest of a lemon or finely chopped	to every lb of apple pulp
lemon rind, and the juice	a few cloves (optional)

Peel and core the apples, boil the peel and cores together with enough water to nearly cover them for 5 minutes. Strain and use this water to boil the peeled, cored and sliced apples in, with the lemon peel and juice. When the apples are cooked, measure the pulp and add 1lb sugar to every pound of apple. Bring the apple and sugar to the boil, simmer for 10 minutes. Pot.

This jam is only good if made with very sharp, tasty cooking apples, as otherwise it is bland. Hardy's cook suggested cooking the apples whole, and then putting them through a sieve, but that is very time-consuming. I think cloves (which she used) overpower the apple. Crab-apples would make good jam but are too fiddly. For them jelly is better.

Crab-apple Jelly

crab-apples	1lb sugar (preserving is best) to
chopped peel of a lemon, and the juice	every pint of juice
	a few cloves or a pinch of ginger
	(optional)

STRAWBERRY PICKERS in CORNICK'S FRUIT-
GARDENS where the famous BRIDPORT
PRESERVES were first made.
From Photo July 1901.
W. G. & F. S. CORNICK.
10. WEST STREET, BRIDPORT.

*In this 1937 advertisement Cornick's
were emphasising their history as jam-
makers. They were Bridport grocers who
started making jam in the 1890s and they
were still advertising the jams and soft
drinks they made in the 1960s.*

Chop the clean crab-apples and boil in enough water to cover them, with the lemon
and spice if used. When soft, strain through a sieve, then strain again through
muslin laid over a sieve (this saves manoeuvring heavy jelly bags). To each pint of
juice add a pound of sugar. Bring to the boil and simmer for 10 minutes. Pot.

Raspberry Jam

Most of Joan Turbeville's recipes are for drying apples, apricots and so on, and are of
little use today. Her raspberry paste, if the Joyce (juice) removal is ignored, makes a
good jam. The original was for a solid preserve:

A RECEIPT TO MACKE RASBERY PASTE
*First Bruse your rasberrys and lett the Joyce run from them then tacke your rasberyes
and put them ovar the fiare and keep sturringe of them about the pann least they
burne untell that you can perceive that theare is noe Joyce in the rasberyes then put
to A powned of your rasberyes dryed A pownde and A quarter of sugar very finely
beaten and sifted and stir it together with a moderate fire that it doth not boyle but
the suge to bee throwley dissolved in it and when it is cowld then put it into mouldes
and dry it in the stoafe.*

Equal quantities of raspberries and preserving sugar, plus 3 tablespoons of lemon juice per lb of fruit. Bring all ingredients slowly to the boil, carefully or else the sugar will burn, and boil for 10 minutes. Pot.

Quince Marmalade

The word jam (sometimes spelt giam) does not enter the language until the late seventeenth or early eighteenth century, and may come from a similar Arab word meaning 'packed tightly together'. Marmalade was the earlier term for what we call jam, and if used alone it meant a quince preserve, not one of oranges. The Tyneham recipe book has several recipes for quince marmalade, including two which are red. One is dyed with barberry juice, the other cooked a long time. Quince marmalade, popular from the medieval period, is now virtually unknown, but is as well worth making as the commoner quince jelly.

From Tyneham:

WHITE QUINCE MARMALADE

Pair quarter and core the Quinces and put them into water and to every Pd of Quinces 3 quarts of a Pd of refined Loaf Sugar put the Quinces into a Skillet and Strew the Sugar on them and let stand a little till the Sugar is dissolved then sett it over the Fire and let in Boil as fast as may be Stiring it and breaking it with a Spoon as it comes from the bottom of the Skillet and is enough don't put in all the Sugar at first and but very little water the juice of grated Quince is better.

Peel and core the quinces, and boil the peelings and cores in enough water to cover them for about 10 minutes. Cut the quince flesh into smallish cubes, and cook until tender in the water strained from the peelings with about 3 tablespoons of lemon juice per pound of fruit. Add 1lb of sugar per pint of pulp, bring to the boil and cook for 10 minutes. Pot.

   If you are short of quinces, or worried about it setting, use ½lb of apple pulp to every pound of quince. The quinces should be ripe, yellow and fragrant.

Mrs Drax's Apricot Marmalade

APRICOCK MARMALADE MRS DRAX

Gather your apricots when ye are dry and not to ripe, wipe ym and take out the Stones, and cut the Spots, but not pare them, take their weight in Duble refine sugar beat very fine Slice your Apricots very thin into your Suger, and to a pound put 5 or 6 Spoonfuls of water boyle it up very Quick, and scum it well, and when it is almost done break your apricocks stones, and put ye kernels into water to blanch them, when they are blanched dry them in a cloth, then put them into the marmalet, and boyle them a quarter of an hour after they are in, when tis a nough put it in pots for use.

Mrs Drax (presumably of Charborough Park) was unusual for her date in not peeling the apricots. She is quite right saying they should not be too ripe: surprisingly, hard apricots made the best jam. Preserving sugar is the best substitute for her double-refined sugar. A popular jam, as the recipe is found in the Bloxworth and Tyneham recipe books in exactly the same words.

an equal quantity of prepared apricots and preserving sugar	2 tablespoons of lemon juice per pound of sugar

Slice the apricots, removing the stones. Heat the apricots and lemon juice together, starting over a low heat. When cooked a little add the sugar. Crack the stones (easiest way is to put them in a piece of cloth, twisted so they can't escape, and hit them with a hammer). Blanch them and remove the skins. Chop into small pieces and add to the jam. Cook for about 10 minutes after the sugar is dissolved. Test for set (a small amount on a cold saucer should form a skin in a few minutes) and put into glass jar, covering with jam tops.

Rhubarb Jam

TO PRESERVE RHUBARB

To 4lbs of Rhubarb cut as for tarts add 3lbs of Pounded loaf sugar, 1oz of bitter almonds blanched and cut into small pieces and peel and Juice of two large lemons. Boil and skin the whole well for ¾ of an hour.

Loose in the family papers of Young of Glanville's Wotton, in an early nineteenth-century hand.

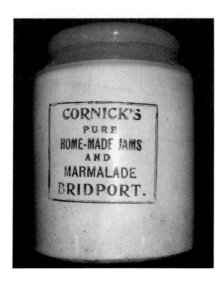

An earthenware pot for Cornick's Home-Made Jams and Marmalade, Bridport. (Bridport Museum)

Miscellaneous

Cheese makers training at the East Stour School, which taught dairy work, c. 1918. Cheese making was becoming more scientific.

Miscellaneous

Furmity

Furmity or frumenty is cooked whole wheat, and is known from the medieval period when it was cooked with meat.

It is famous because of Hardy: in *The Mayor of Casterbridge* the hero was steered away from the beer tent at the fair, into one which sold furmity. There 'a haggish creature of about fifty presided. She slowly stirred the contents of the pot. The dull scrape of her large spoon was audible throughout the tent as she thus kept from the burning the mixture of corn in the grain, milk, raisins, currants, and what not, that composed the antiquated slop in which she dealt . . . [Furmity] . . . was as proper a food as could be obtained within four seas though, to those not accustomed to it, the grains of wheat swollen as large as lemon pips, which floated on it surface, might have had a deterrent effect at first'. The hero manages to get drunk on the rum the furmity woman adds to the mixture.

Basically furmity is a sort of whole wheat porridge. I tried it according to the recipe below, and although the wheat was soft after cooking, it tasted of very little. Unlike oats porridge the wheat did not merge with the milk. After the addition of fruit and spices it was perfectly edible, but not very exciting.

> FOR FOUR PEOPLE
> 4 tablespoons whole wheat
> milk
> cinnamon, mace, dried fruit

Soak the wheat overnight in water, drain and simmer in enough milk to cover it for an hour. It burns easily. After simmering it should be soft and have burst its skins. Older recipes suggest a couple of spoonfuls of sugar should be added, but if a little dried fruit and powered spice is added it is sweet enough.

Mrs Caddy, Thomas Hardy's housekeeper, gave the following recipe to Paul Nash:

> Half a pint of wheat   Half a pound of raisins (whole,
> Half a pound of currants   not stoned)
>   Two quarts of milk

The wheat is boiled in water until tender, and the currants and raisins boiled separately. Bring the milk almost to the boil, add the wheat 'and let it get thoroughly cooked'. Add the raisins and currants and let it simmer for 3 hours or more; add sugar (or spice).

Tess milking by Vivien Gribble, 1926.

Cheese

> Wi all his meal ov woone dry crust
> An' Vinny cheese so dry as doust
> > William Barnes, 1859

The Blackmoor Vale and the river valleys of south and west Dorset are famous dairying areas, but more famous for butter than cheese. Stevenson's agricultural report of 1815 said 'there is little or no *raw-milk* [i.e. whole milk] cheese made in the county. Some of the Skim-milk cheese, which is called by way of ridicule, *double Dorset*, is streaked with a kind of blue mould [said to be made] by breaking and sprinkling the curds with flour after they have been pressed'.

The name blue vinney does not seem to have been used then. Vinney means mouldy in the Dorset dialect and William Barnes also recorded 'Ha'skim' as the Dorset name for half-skimmed cheese, cheese made from milk skimmed once.

In the early 1860s an American who walked from London to Land's End and back had the dairying of the Blackmoor Vale explained to him by local farmers who made some cheese from partly skimmed milk, producing a good cheese. 'Then there is a certain quantity of the genuine old-fashioned, skimmed cheese, made of milk which has given up to the butter-churn every iota of cream in it, before it goes to the press. This is an article well known in New England . . . known as *white-oak cheese*, owing to its solidity. Softer missiles have been fired with great effect from cannon.' (*A Walk from London to Land's End and Back* (1865) by Elihu Burritt)

Paul Nash in his Shell *Guide* of 1936 thought blue vinney 'one of those interesting cheeses which the English counties produce for their inhabitants, but which are seldom eaten by anyone but continental connoisseurs'.

Victor MacClure, a self-confessed gourmand, sampled blue vinney in the 1950s, describing it as 'a skim-milk cheese which, properly kept, develops a blue veining and a particularly individual flavour. It can, however, assume a consistency like celluloid, and be rather a bad cheese. I think the cause of this extraction of too much of the cream by the separator. But when you find the farmer who possibly restores some of the cream to the skim-milk intended for cheese-making, and if he knows how to bring the cheese to maturity, it wants a lot of beating.'

Others who ate the cheese agree that it was hard, and it generally ceased being made in the late 1950s. It is now available again.

Dorset Blue is cheaper than 'Fine Best Cheese' in this advertisement of 1905.

Tyneham Cheesecake

A RICH CURD CHEESE CAKE (TYNEHAM)

2 pd of fine cheese Curd drain'd clean from the Whey, a pd of butter rub ym together though a hair sieve add the ylks of six eggs half a pd of white Sugar, A pd currents a nutmeg and pennyworth of Cinnamon beat the Eggs with Rose water and a pretty deal of sack, bake ym half an hour.

8oz curd cheese	pastry case
4oz butter or margarine	4oz currants; cinnamon and nutmeg;
2oz caster sugar	rose water; sherry (optional)
2 egg yolks	

Mix the curd cheese, butter (or margarine) and sugar together, add the egg yolks (with a tablespoon of rose water, a pinch of cinnamon and nutmeg, currants or a tablespoon of sherry, if wanted). It is best to partly pre-cook the pastry case, blind, for 15 minutes at gas mark 6. Then put the filling in (it will expand, so allow room) and bake at gas mark 4 for 35 to 45 minutes. The filling will set. Use any extra filling for small tarts, and cook for 20–25 minutes.

Very good plain, when it is worth using butter, and very good spicy, when it is not. Currants plump up and are a good addition. In the medieval period elderflowers were added, about 2 tablespoons to 8oz cheese. If in a hurry, the filling and pastry case can be cooked together at gas mark 6 for about 45 minutes, but this can make the under pastry a little soggy.

Polly Lock ready to milk, c. 1910.

Dorset Food Today

Over the last twenty years we have become much more interested in where our food comes from. Organic and local produce is valued, and is now easily purchased. Local produce is sold at farmers' markets; specialist shops in towns; the weekly markets in the towns; Women's Institute markets and National Trust shops. Roadside stalls often offer local produce. There are many more farm shops, and several towns and villages have very good bakeries.

FARMERS' MARKETS

There are monthly farmers' markets at Blandford, Bridport, Christchurch, Corfe, Dorchester, Gillingham, Shaftesbury, Sherborne, Sturminster Newton, Wareham and Wimborne, and new ones are being set up all the time. See the Tourist Information Offices for dates.

WOMEN'S INSTITUTE MARKETS

The WI have weekly produce markets in Bridport (Sat a.m.); Christchurch (Mon a.m.); Dorchester (Fri a.m.); Gillingham (Fri a.m.); Portland (Fri a.m.); Shaftesbury (Thurs a.m.); Sherborne (Thurs a.m.); Sturminster Newton (Mon a.m.); Swanage (Fri a.m.); Verwood (Fri a.m.); Wimborne (Fri a.m.) and Wool (Thurs a.m.).

Information on farmers' markets from www.dorsetfoodlinks.co.uk;
on WI markets from www.wimarkets.co.uk.
For local food see www.tasteofthewest.co.uk; www.directfromdorset.org.uk

Farm Shops

Farm shops usually offer their own produce alongside a wide selection from other local producers. Most of them have fruit, vegetables, cheese, ice cream, meat and jams. This is the most efficient way for the shopper to see a wide range of local produce, and indeed produce from adjacent counties. This book concentrates entirely on Dorset, but much of the county is close to Devon, Somerset, Wiltshire or Hampshire and these counties also produce good food.

The idea of visiting small shops can be off-putting because we are all so used to supermarkets. Do not be put off: the shops are friendly, informative and do not pressurise you to buy. Seasonal fruit and vegetables, and close association between the animals and the meat, are unfamiliar to us too, but very healthy.

For food events like Bridport Food Week and current farmers' markets see the Tourist Information Offices or the local press.

Picking watercress at Doddings, Bere Regis, 1930s. (Jesty collection)

Chip basket for Dorset watercress, designed in about 1900. (Jesty collection)

MILK, CHEESE . . . AND ICE CREAM

Organic milk and cream is readily available, and in the Bride Valley even the rich Jersey versions. Local ice cream, some of it organic, is sold in many shops and is delicious. Dorset Blue Vinney is being made again, along with very good and widely distributed Cheddars. Specialist cheeses are also made including goats' milk cheeses, and yoghurts from goat or sheep milk. Local butter is available.

MEAT

Locally produced and organic mean can be purchased direct from farmers and from shops. Many butchers in the towns have local meat, as do most of the farm shops. Beef, lamb and pork are the most frequent, but mutton and rarer breeds are also on sale along with sausages and local bacon.

VEGETABLES, SALADS AND FRUIT

Farmers' markets and shops have a wide range of seasonal vegetables and salads, and there are a few pick-your-own farms in the county. Blueberries are grown in Dorset, a surprising crop. Hot chillis and peppers are also unexpected. Dorset's traditional

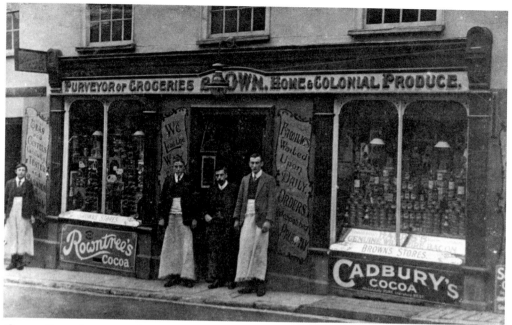

George Brown's grocery shop, Lyme Regis, c. 1910. (Lyme Regis Museum)

orchards were mostly for cider (still made here) but there are a couple of orchard areas in west Dorset. Jam is made locally, and of course local honey is on sale.

FISH
Most Dorset markets and seaside towns have people selling locally caught fish, although shellfish can be more difficult as much is exported. Oysters are a speciality at Smallmouth, Portland. Smoked fish (and meat, cheese, etc.) is produced at Bridport, and Dorset has trout farms.

FLOUR, DORSET KNOBS, ETC.
Stoneground wholemeal flour is made in Dorset, and widely available through health food shops and farm shops. Dorset knobs are still made in the traditional way at Morecombelake, along with a wide range of sweet biscuits. Dorset is lucky in having good local bakeries.

SUPPLIERS
Suppliers change all the time – opening, moving and sometimes closing. This list is from mid-2006, and will be wrong very soon thereafter. For more details of suppliers see the book *Eat Dorset* (2005) by Michael Feasey. Most of those listed supply organic food. Some only sell by post or to order – those with shops are indicated.

Fruit and veg, etc.
Ansty PYO and Farm Shop
Ansty
Tel: 01747 829072
Web: www.anstypyo.co.uk

Shop: butcher's, local produce and own bacon
R.J. Balson and Son
9 West Allington
Bridport
DT6 5BJ
Tel: 01308 422638

Free-range eggs
Becklands Farm
Becklands Lane
Whitchurch Canonicorum
Bridport
DT6 6RG
Tel: 01297 560298
Email
becklandsorganicfarm@btopenworld.com

Squashes, vegetables, etc.
Bothen Hill Produce
7 Green Lane
Bothenhampton
Bridport
DT6 4ED
Tel: 01308 424271
Web: www.bothenhillproduce.co.uk

Bride Valley Garlic Ltd
Outlook Farm
Litton Cheney
Dorchester
DT2 9BA
Tel: 01308 482108

Shop: kippers, smoked trout, chicken, etc.
Bridfish Smokery
Unit 1
The Old Laundry Industrial Estate

Sea Road North
Bridport
DT6 3BD
Tel: 01308 456306

Bridport Centre for Local Food
17 St Michael's Trading Estate
Foundry lane
Bridport
DT6 3RR
Tel: 01308 420260
Web: www.foodandland.org

Shop: meat, veg, etc. (Thur p.m.; Fri and Sat a.m.)
Cannings Court Organic Farm Shop
Cannings Court
Pulham
Dorchester
DT2 7EA
Tel: 01258 818035

Turkeys, chicken, geese, etc.
W.J. Chilcott and Co.
Glebe Farm
Owermoigne
Dorchester
DT2 8HN
Tel: 01305 852639

Pork by post
Childhay Manor Organics
Childhay
Blackdown
Beaminster
DT8 3LQ
Tel: 01308 868709

Shop: own organic chocolate (closed Sun)
Chococo
Commercial Road
Swanage
BH19 1DF
Web: www.chococo.co.uk

Cheeses

Cranborne Chase Cheese
The Estate Office
Manor Farm
Ashmore
Nr. Salisbury
SP5 5AE
Tel: 01747 811125
Email: manorfarmashmore@waitrose.com

Shop: fish and shellfish

Davy's Locker
The Old Mill
Priory Lane
Bridport
DT6 3RW
Tel: 01308 456131

Cheese, butter, bacon, etc.

Denhay Farms
Broadoak
Bridport
DT6 5NP
Tel: 01308 458963
Web: www.denhay.co.uk

Blueberries and juice

The Dorset Blueberry Company
Littlemoors Farm
Ham Lane
Hampreston
Wimborne
B21 7LX
Tel: 01202 579342
Web: www.dorset-blueberry.co.uk

Dorset Blue Vinney
Woodbridge Farm
Stock Gaylard
Sturminster Newton
DT10 2BD
Tel: 01963 23216
Web: www.dorsetblue.com

Shop: lamb, beef, bacon, veg, etc. (Fri only)

Downhouse Farm
Higher Eype
Bridport
DT6 6AH
Tel: 01308 421232

The Village Bakery
18 Fore Street
Evershot
Dorchester
DT2 0JW
Tel: 01935 83379

Shop: meat (weekends and school hols)

Eggardon Rare Breeds
Hill Barn Farm
Kingston Russell
DT2 9ED
Tel: 01308 482491
Web: www.eggardon.co.uk

Shop: beef, mutton, lamb, eggs, veg, etc.

Eweleaze Farm
Osmington Hill
Osmington
DT3 6ED
Tel: 01305 833690
Web: www.eweleaze.co.uk

Shop, café. Oysters and other seafood

Fleet Oyster Farm and Crab House Café
Ferryman's Way
Weymouth
DT4 9YU
Tel: 01305 788867

Cheeses – small shop

Ford Farm
Ashley Chase Estates
Park Farm
Litton Cheney
Dorchester
DT2 9AZ
Web: www.fordfarm.com

Fudges
Dorset Village Bakery Limited
Pinesway Business Park
Station Road
Stalbridge
DT10 2RN
Tel: 01963 362402
Web: www.fudges.co.uk

Shop: beef, pork etc. (Tues–Sat p.m. only)
Green Lane Farm Shop
Manor Farm
Hooke
DT8 3PB
Tel: 01308 863817

Shop and café: meat, dairy, veg, etc. (Wed–Sun)
Gold Hill Organic Farm Shop
Ridgeway Lane
Child Okeford
Blandford Forum
DT11 8HB
Tel: 01258 861413
Web: www.thegreenhouse.biz

Large shop – great variety of meat, eggs, veg, dairy, etc.
Goldy's Farm Shop
West Holme
Wareham
BH20 6AQ
Tel: 01929 556777
Web: www.goldys.co.uk

Green Valley Organic Farm Shop (Wed–Sat)
Long Meadow
Godmanstone
DT2 7AE
Tel: 01300 342164

Organic pork
Heritage Prime@Shedbush Farm
Muddy Ford Lane
Stanton St Gabriel

Bridport
DT6 6DR
Tel: 01297 489304
Web: www.heritageprime.co.uk

Large shop – great variety of meat, eggs, veg, dairy (Tue–Sat)
Home Farm Shop
Tarrant Gunville
Blandford Forum
DT11 8JW

Cakes, etc.
Honeybuns
Naish Farm
Stony Lane
Holwell
Sherborne
DT9 5JL
Tel: 01963 23597
Web: www.honeybuns.co.uk

Shop: great variety
Logan Farm Shop
Orchard Park Garden Centre
Gillingham
SP8 5JG
Tel: 01747 835021
Web: www.orchardpark.biz

Shop: bread, cakes, buns, etc.
Leakers Bakery
29 East Street
Bridport
DT6 3JX
Tel: 01308 423296

Shop: wood-fired breads, buns, etc. (closed Mon)
Long Crichel Bakery
Long Crichel
Wimborne
B21 5JU
Tel: 01258 830852
Web: www.longcrichelbakery.co.uk

Organic fruit and vegetables
Long Crichel Organic Garden
Long Crichel
Wimborne
BH21 5JU
Tel: 01258 830295
Email: longcrichelgarden@cooptel.net

**Shop: meat etc. (closed Mon, Thurs; open p.m.
  only Tues, Wed, Fri)**
Longburton Farm Shop
Longburton
Sherborne
DT9 5PG
Tel: 01963 210203

Small shop: organic milk and cream
Manor Farm Organic Dairy
Godmanstone
Dorchester
DT2 7AH
Tel: 01300 341415
Web: www.manor-farm-organic.co.uk

Shop: Jersey milk, cream, veg, meat
Modbury Farm
Burton Bradstock
Bridport
DT6 4NE
Tel: 01308 897193
Web: www.modburyfarm.com

Shop: knobs, biscuits, etc.
S Moores
Morcombelake
Nr Bridport
DT6 6ES
Tel: 01297 489753
Web: www.moores-biscuits.co.uk

Asparagus and fruit
Oakland's Plantation
Coldharbour
Wareham
B20 7PA
Tel: 01929 554929

Trout and seafish
Organic and Wild
Golden Springs Farm
Waddock Cross
Bere Regis
Tel: 01300 320640
Web: www.organicwild.co.uk

Shop: pork, lamb and great variety
Pampered Pigs
Rye Hill Farmhouse
Rye Hill
Bere Regis
Wareham
BH20 7LP
Tel: 01929 472327
Web: www.pampered-pigs.co.uk

Peppers and chillies
Peppers by Post
Sea Spring Farm
West Bexington
Dorchester
DT2 9DD
Tel: 01308 897892
Web: www.peppersbypost.biz

Ice cream
Purbeck Ice Cream
Lower Scoles Farm
Kingston
Wareham
BH20 5LG
Tel: 01929 480090
Web: www.purbeckicecream.co.uk

Veg, sauces, ice cream, etc.
Rural Foods
Lower Woolcombe Farm
Melbury Bubb
Dorchester
DT2 0NJ
Tel: 01935 83168
Web: www.ruralfoods.co.uk

Scallops etc.
Shellseekers
Ten Acres
Conygar
Broadmayne
Dorchester
DT2 8LX
Tel: 08074 104607

Shop: meat and veg (Fri a.m. and Sat a.m.)
Star Farm
Hazelbury Bryan
Dorset
DT10 2EG
Tel: 01258 817285

Large shop – great variety. Café
Stevens Farm Shop
Martinstown
Dorchester
DT2 9JR
Tel: 01305 889216

Flour and veg
N.R. Stoate and Sons
Cann Mills
Shaftesbury
SP7 0BL
Tel: 01747 852475
Web: www.stoatesflour.co.uk

The Strawberry Patch
Andy Brown
Crepe Farm Business Park
Symondsbury
Bridport
DT6 6EY
Tel: 07941 583497

Shop: veg, meat, dairy, fruit
Sturts Farm Community
Sheiling Trust
Three Cross Road

West Moors
Ferndown
BH22 0NF

Shop: beef, lamb, etc.; seasonal veg and salad
Sunnyside Organic Farm
Lower Kingcombe
Toller Porcorum
Dorchester
DT2 0EQ
Tel: 01300 321537

A wide range
Sydling Brook Organic Farm Shop
Up Sydling
Dorchester
DT2 9PG
Tel: 01300 341992
Web: www.sydling.co.uk

Shop: veg, salads (Tues a.m., Fri p.m.)
Tamarisk Farm
West Bexington
Dorchester
DT2 9DF
Tel: 01308 897781
Web: www.tamariskfarm.com

Breads and sometimes flour
The Town Mill Bakery
Mill Lane
Lyme Regis
DT7 3PU
Tel: 01297 444033
Web: www.townmill.org.uk

Shop, café: great variety
The Udder Farm Shop
East Stour
Gillingham
SP8 5LQ
Tel: 01747 838899

Shop: meat, etc. (closed Sun and Mon)
Twelve Green Acres
Organic Farm Shop
Lytchett Minster
Poole
BH16 6AP
Tel: 01202 631044
Web: www.12green acres.co.uk

Large shop: own veg and many local
   suppliers
Washingpool Farm Shop and Restaurant
North Allington
Bridport
DT6 5HP
Tel: 01308 459549
Web: www.washingpool.co.uk

Lamb, mutton
Westleaze Farm
Whitesheet Hill
Beaminster
DT8 3SF
Tel: 01308 861408

Sheep and goat's milk yoghurts
Woodlands Park Dairy
Woodlands
Wimborne
BH21 8LX
Tel: 01202 822687
Web: www.woodlands-park.co.uk

Goat's milk cheese, etc.
Woolsery Cheese
The Old Dairy
Up Sydling
Dorchester
DT2 9PQ
Tel: 01300 341991
Web: www.woolserycheese.co.uk

Lamb, sausages, etc.
Wyld Meadow Lamb
Wyld Meadow Farm
Monkton Wyld
Bridport
DT6 6DD
Tel: 01297 678318

Twin calves, much rarer then, on a Dorset farm in the 1920s.

Rosebrand Creamery, Dorchester, with vegetable allotments behind, in the 1920s.

Bibliography

THE DORSET COOKERY BOOKS

Joan Turbeville's recipe book for fruits is in the Parnham papers, and the later pages were used as an account book in the 1670s. She was born at Chantmarle in 1622 and married John Turbeville of Woolbridge in 1640. Since her book remained with her parent's family – the Strodes – it was presumably written before her marriage. The papers are kept in Dorset Record Office, D1/MW/F3.

A selection of Mary Chafin's recipes, dating from around the 1690s, were published in 1979 as *Mary Chafin's Country Recipes*. She was born at Chettle in 1680, married in 1698, moved to Pucknowle Manor in 1709 and died in 1719. The original manuscript is in private hands.

The large volume inscribed on the first page 'Mrs Machen 1709' comes from Bloxworth, and must have been used there in the time of the Trenchards. Who Mrs Machen was is not certain. Even the extensive notes by W.A. Pickard-Cambridge about Bloxworth in the Dorset County Museum do not mention the name. The main part of the book dates from 1709, but there are many later additions. The book is in Dorset Record Office, D1/OA/F1.

Also from Bloxworth is a mid- to late eighteenth-century volume, again with many additions. There are several recipes written as part of, or on the back of, letters written to Mrs Pickard at Bloxworth, and it was probably started by Henrietta Trenchard, whose husband, Jocelyn Pickard, bought Bloxworth in 1753. She died aged 71 as her severely classical memorial in Bloxworth church records. This too is in Dorset Record Office, D60/F74.

The Tyneham recipe book has provided by far the greatest number of recipes. It is certainly eighteenth century, probably the second half of that century. A medicinal recipe in the book is dated 1768, and 'An account of what is now in the House', found loose in the book, is dated 1763. These dates would fit well with the variety of recipes found and would mean that the recipe book belonged to Margaret, a daughter of John Williams of Herringston. She married John Bond of Tyneham in 1715 and died in 1775. However the Bond family, in particular Mrs L.M.G. Bond who did so much work on the family history, have always thought it belonged to Jane Biggs, who married the Revd William Bond in 1794. The recipe book was kindly lent to me by Major General H.M.G. Bond, their great-great-grandson.

The Sadborow recipe book belonged to a Bragge daughter of the big house, in Thorncombe parish, west Dorset. It was kindly given to me by Jenny Roger, and is now in the Dorset Record Office. Recipes dated 1819, 1808 and 1813 occur in the front parts of the book, and one dated 1831 is pinned in the back. This Sadborow book has many recipes for curry and pilaw (pilau), showing a strong Indian influence.

In a collection of material from Blandford St Mary is a recipe book of about 1810, whose history is uncertain. Judging by the variety of raw materials used and so on I believe it to be from Dorset, and it is in Dorset Record Office, D176/25.

Dairying country in Dorset from a wood engraving by Vivien Gribble for the 1926 edition of Tess of the D'Urbervilles.

Offering fish from baskets at Bridport, 1890s. (Bridport Museum)

The Piddletrenthide recipe book dates from around 1824 with additions up to the twentieth century, and comes from the Bridge family, one of whom, John Bridge, became a well-known London silversmith, a partner in the large firm of silversmiths, Rundell, Bridge and Rundell. He died in 1834 and so perhaps ate dishes prepared from the book, which is in Dorset Record Office, D1031.

There are two mid-nineteenth-century recipe books from Bloxworth: the one used here belonged to T.G. Theobald and is dated 1854. She was a relative of the Pickard-Cambridges. In Dorset Record Office D60/F54.

The Farmer's Loaf comes from a manuscript cookery book belonging to Ellen M. Edwards, probably from Bridport, which is dated 1917 and has several wartime shortage recipes, e.g. for vegetarian sausages and 'mock' fish of ground rice. In Dorset Record Office D/BTM/F4/1.

A few of the recipes in this book are to be found in *Dorset Dishes of the 18th Century* (1961) and *Dorset Dishes of the 17th Century* (1967), both edited by J. Stevens Cox. The Bragge family recipes are from the latter.

Dorset Recipes (not dated, 1960s), published by the WI, has several Dorset apple cake recipes and other traditional fare, some of which are included in *Dorset Dishes* (1979) by Kate Easlea. The Portland Dough Cake recipes are from letters to *Dorset* (no. 7, 22 and no. 9, 25; 1969) and the Sherborne Stodger from Katherine Barker.

For Cornick's jam factory, see *Dorset County Chronicle*, 16 July 1948.

COOKERY BOOKS
Ellis, William, *The Country Housewife's Family Companion* (1750)
MacClure, Victor, *Good Appetite My Companion* (1955)
White, Florence, *Good Things in England* (1932)

MEMOIRS
Anon [Jane Ellen Panton], *Fresh Leaves and Green Pastures* (1909)
Darton, F.J.H., *The Marches of Wessex* (1922)
Egerton, Blanche, *Some Recollections of Early Days* (West Stafford) DRO D500/28
Horsfall, Mary, *Life in Bridport 1898–1918* (1969)
Joyce, H.S., *I Was Born in the Country* (1946)
O'Keefe, John, *Recollections of John O'Keefe* (1826)
Powys, Llewelyn, *Wessex Memories* (2003)
Wightman, Ralph, *Moss Green Days* (1947)

HISTORY
The Marn'll Book (1952)
The Casebook of Sir Francis Ashley JP Recorder of Dorchester 1614–35, edited by J.H. Bettey (1981)
Hutchins, John, *The History and Antiquities of the County of Dorset* (1774);
also used: 2nd edn vol. 1, 1796, and Richard Pultney's *Natural History Notes* attached to 2nd edn vol. 3, 1813
Udal, J.S., *Dorsetshire Folk-lore* (1922)

A handsome display of hams at Boon's grocery shop, Dorchester, c. 1912.

Real and tinned fruit displayed at Boon's, possiby for the 1911 coronation.

Victoria History of the County of Dorset, vol. 2 (1908)

Wood-Legh, K.C., *A Small Household of the XVth century being the account book of Munden's Chantry, Bridport* (1956)

AGRICULTURE

Marshall, Mr, *The Rural Economy of the West of England* (1796)

Stevenson, William, *General View of the Agriculture of the County of Dorset* (1815)

THE LABOURERS

Eden, Sir F.M., *The State of the Poor* (1797)

1843 *Report of the Assistant Poor Law Commissioners on the Employment of Women and Children in Agriculture*

1867 *Royal Commission into the Employment of Children, Young Persons and Women in Agriculture*

Manuscript: John Bright's notebook, *c.* 1844, in Dorset County Library E.C. Tufnell's Report on the State of the Labourers in Dorset, *c.* 1844 British Museum Add. MS 40587, f.182

WEYMOUTH

Broadley, A.M., *Royal Weymouth 1789–1805*, in Weymouth Library (1907)

Ellis, George, *A History of Weymouth* (1829)

HARDY AND LAWRENCE

Eet, Miss, *The Domestic Life of Thomas Hardy* (1963)

The letters of T.E. Lawrence of Arabia edited by David Garnett (1964)

T.E. Lawrence by his friends (1947)

Mitchell, Annie, *Cook at Max Gate* (1970)

Titterington, Ellen E., *Afterthoughts of Max Gate* (1969)

FOOD

David, Elizabeth, *English Bread and Yeast Cookery* (1977)

Eilson, C. Anne, *Food and Drink in Britain* (1973)

Grigson, Jane, *Fish Cookery* (1973)

Grigson, Jane, *English Food* (1974)

Index

Recipes in italic

157

Butcher's stall in the covered market in Dorchester in the very early twentieth century – full of imported New Zealand lamb.

HEWLETT & SON,
FISHMONGERS, POULTERERS, AND GAME SALESMAN,
WEST STREET, BLANDFORD, and at Leadenhall and Billingsgate Markets, London.

Rough Wenham Lake Ice. **Pure Cod Liver Oil.**

A goodly array of fish in a Blandford advertisement of 1875.